TIMOTHÉE CHALAMET

An Unauthorized Biography

DAMIEN CARLISLE

POST Hill
PRESS

A POST HILL PRESS BOOK

ISBN: 978-1-64293-116-7
ISBN (eBook): 978-1-64293-117-4

Timothée Chalamet:
An Unauthorized Biography

Cover design by Cody Corcoran
Cover photo by Elena Ringo

Post Hill Press, LLC
New York • Nashville
posthillpress.com

Published in the United States of America

CONTENTS

INTRODUCTION

A New Crop of Ambition

Timothée Chalamet. It is a name that could *perhaps* go down in history as the greatest actor of our time. That's quite a statement to live up to wouldn't you say? Tom Hanks, Jack Nicholson, Marlon Brando, Robert De Niro…undeniably great actors who will go down in history among the premier male actors of the 20th century. *Citizen Kane, The Godfather, Psycho.* All films from the 20th century that need no explanation.

These classics shaped and molded how we view movies—and how stories are told, for that matter—today. Film, as we know it now, would be vastly different if we hadn't made such leaps and bounds in storytelling, film technology, editing, and casting throughout the 20th century. For example, films shot from varying angles in one scene—a technique that helps the viewer feel as if they are standing in the room with the characters—brings the story to life. The movies that you have lined up across your shelves in your home would not only still be in black and white, but they would be about ninety seconds long and have no sound at all.

Our love for the connection between reality and fiction, the connection that we have to fictitious characters, would be just a pipedream, or somewhat of a fairytale. Their ability to reach into our chest and make us feel the same physical and heart-wrenching emotional pain would be nonexistent without the drive by so many of these actors, directors, and crew, to make this craft as great as it is today.

Stories have developed into intricate plots that tug at the heartstrings, reminding us of something we've experienced or suffered through. We relate to these stories, to these characters. We are reminded that we are not alone, that our experiences are not unique. From the timing to the writing, to the very sounds that propel everything forward, the men and women of the film industry have the art form nailed down to a science. They know how to make a classic film that can grab the viewer and leave them yearning for more.

But what is a film without characters? And what is a character without an actor to bring it to life? Who is going to bring the humanistic quality to the screen? How can we, as viewers, relate to a continuous thread of images strung together at rapid speed? Actors make characters relatable, indulgent, and furthermore, *human*.

However, ladies and gentlemen, this is no longer the 20th century. We are witnessing, once again, a shift of generations. The independent film industry is overflowing with wide-eyed, eager, passionate young people, each of them ready to storm the industry.

- **Trey Edward Shults**, for example, is a mere twenty-nine years old and has already been awarded numerous accolades, namely his film *Krisha* winning the Grand Jury Award at SXSW 2015, and his post-apocalyptic horror film *It Comes at Night* (2017) has been positively received by film critics.
- **Xavier Dolan**, Canadian actor, writer, director, and producer, is also the ripe young age of twenty-nine. His film *It's Only the End of the World* won awards at Cannes in 2016 and was selected as the Canadian entry for the Best Foreign Language Film at the 89th Academy Awards.
- **Saoirse Ronan**, according to the actress herself her name is pronounced 'sur-sha,' and this Irish-American actress, at the age of twenty-four, has already garnered a Golden Globe Award, three Academy Award nominations, and four British Academy Film Award nominations.
- **Ansel Elgort**, attendee of LaGuardia High School of Music & Art and Performing Arts; portrayed Caleb Prior in The Divergent Series franchise, Augustus Waters in the romantic teen drama *The Fault in Our Stars* (2014), and the title character in Edgar Wright's action thriller *Baby Driver* (2017), for which he received a Golden Globe nomination for Best Actor in a Motion Picture.
- **Emma Watson** rose to fame in J.K. Rowling's *Harry Potter* series as Hermione Granger, but at age twenty-eight, she is so much more; earned praise for leading role in *The Perks of Being a Wallflower* (2012), receiving an MTV Movie

Award, a Teen Choice Award, and a People's
Choice Award; she also starred as Belle in the
2017 feature *Beauty and the Beast.*

The experiences differing from generation to generation
offer a deep pool of new material, emotions, and relationship
dynamics to pull from. No matter how society changes, one
thing remains timeless—*human nature.* The desperate need
for approval, love, acceptance. The deep ache for drama, conflict, strife. Sometimes we are slow to admit it, yet all these
traits are very much human.

What will the new crop of ambition bring to our living
rooms and local theatres? Will it be all that we are hoping it
to be? Will it bring us back to our high school years when we
were young and oh-so-naïve? Will we feel emotions we forgot
we could feel, thanks to fresh new portrayals and formats and
faces? The future of film is promising indeed.

Who Is Timothée Chalamet, Really?

Timothée Chalamet is swiftly becoming one of the leaders
among passionate and promising young film stars. In this
book, we'll discuss who this new player on the set is and how
he grew up, then we'll delve further into his early films and
breakout roles. Finally, we'll look to the future and speculate
how far Timothée's star will rise.

Before we do any of that, however, why should we care?
Who is this Timothée Chalamet?

Talking about a twenty-two-year-old actor, when the
timeline of his work is manifestly much shorter, makes it a
bit tough to discuss the journey his career has taken. After all,
he only has a few years of work behind him. Yet Timothée

Chalamet, a New York actor, has managed to fit quite a bit into a brief decade, and what he has accomplished is dissimilar to what many expect of American 'child' actors. Timothée didn't do the usual audition circuit in L.A. like so many actors his age, which seems to have helped him ward off the strife that often plagues those working in film while so young. Timothée did a few TV ads, then he attended the Fiorello H. LaGuardia High School, where he learned how acting should be treated as a 'craft.'

His drama training was largely undertaken at the highschool level. He did do a year at Columbia, but then transferred to the Gallatin School of Individualized Study to give more time to his career. This lends Timothée an air of precocity and professionalism seldom found in most of his contemporaries. Certainly, raw talent must also be there, but doing the actual work of studying one's craft has myriad benefits. Indeed, by the time Timothée became a full-time actor, he'd already exercised his discipline in full-time dramatic education. This included starring in school productions of *Cabaret* and *Sweet Charity*, in addition to an obligatory *Law & Order* job. He'd even made his Off Broadway debut, receiving rave reviews. In so doing all this, Timothée had prepared himself for the 'grind' without experiencing the burnout.

He went on to act in some short horrors, did a stint on *Homeland*, then made his major movie debut with the critically reviled *Men, Women & Children*, a.k.a. Jason Reitman's banal disputation on how the internet is bad. Its failure, fortunately for Timothée, was eclipsed by the success of his next release in that same year, Christopher

Nolan's *Interstellar*, where he played the younger version of Casey Affleck's character.

Up until his breakthrough in 2017, Timothée's film-ography is a provocative portfolio of mainly indie efforts alternating with something a little more mainstream here and there, but by and large there are no technicolor kiddie films, no Disney Channel shows, nothing that might cause him to cringe or regret his early work at some point later in life. To date, in fact, his portfolio comes across as that of an established character actor rather than a kid working his way into movies. As talented as he is, it's improbable he had the miraculous foresight to work such thespian thau-maturgy, as acting is as much luck as it is opportunity— Timothée would be one of the first to agree—however, it helps feed into the image of him as a person wise beyond their years. He's not simply some fine young actor, he's nigh untouchable. Even Timothée's bad work isn't *bad* per se. He's obviously young, yes, but his talent is at such a level beyond his age that, in most regards, he never strikes one as merely "a kid."

In 2017, Timothée had a meteoric rise. He became an irrefutable, award-winning film star almost overnight. He had supporting roles in Christian Bale's *Hostiles* and Greta Gerwig's renowned directorial debut, *Lady Bird*, then his indie drama entitled *Hot Summer Nights* played well at South by Southwest, but what set it all off at the beginning of the year was the Sundance premiere of Luca Guadagnino's *Call Me by Your Name*. The film was an immediate critical hit, staying apace with its fervent buzz the duration of 2017 from January to December—quite a rarity in this business. Standing ovations followed *CMBYN* from festival to festival. Timothée became heralded as Hollywood's new "golden boy." Nearly every review of his performance imparts the same star-making narrative: Timothée Chalamet is a once in a generation talent.

EARLY LIFE

Showbiz Family

Timothée Hal Chalamet was born to Nicole Flender and Marc Chalamet on an icy but clear-skied[1] December 27, 1995. He was born into a "showbiz" family. His mother had grown up with performance as her passion and the arts—acting, dancing, her love for French literature—ingrained within her soul. Nicole attended LaGuardia and graduated cum laude from Yale. She danced at Lincoln Center with the New York City Ballet as a child and went on to perform in numerous Broadway musicals including *A Chorus Line, Fiddler on the Roof, Gypsy, Hello Dolly!,* and *My One and Only,* among others.[2]

Nicole's father, Harold Flender, was a screenwriter and is known for *Rescue in Denmark* (1963), a World War II Holocaust rescue novel,[3] and the films *Paris Blues* (1961) and *I Spy* (1955). He also wrote for Sid Caesar (as did Woody Allen, Mel Brooks, and Carl Reiner) for *The Jackie Gleason Show* in the 1950s. Thus, Nicole and her brother, Rodman, were born and raised in the movie business. (Rodman, by the way, is mistakenly referred to in several online sources as Robin Flender. Someone misheard Timothée in an interview, and it has proliferated. His uncle's name is indeed Rodman, named after their mother's maiden name, Enid Rodman.)

Like Nicole, Rodman—*not Robin*—followed in their father's footsteps, too, as a screenwriter, actor, director, and producer. His works include directing multiple episodes of *The Office, Ugly Betty, Chicago Hope, Gilmore Girls, The O.C.,* HBO's *Tales from the Crypt, Finding Carter,* and *Scream* (the TV series). Rodman also married Amy Lippman, a screenwriter and television producer of shows such as *Party of Five, Time of Your Life,* and *House Hunting.*

So, the Force of show business is Strong with Timothée Chalamet. He has it, his mother, uncle, and aunt have it. And his slightly older sister, Pauline, has it—yes, she's taken the thespian path, currently lives in Paris, and has been featured in short films *Between Fear and Laughter* (2016) and *Agnès et Milane* (2017). And while their mother has put aside her ballet career, she remains active with her family and is also a successful real estate broker, an author (writing for *The Boston Herald, The Ottawa Citizen,* and *The Daily Oklahoman*), and an officer of the Actors' Equity Association.

Oh, yes. Timothée's father, Marc Chalamet, is no slouch either. Of French descent, he works as an editor for UNICEF and for the United Nations, and it's said he spoke to his children in French, giving both Timothée and Pauline an ear for multiple languages from an early age and a unique way of being raised.

Hell's Kitchen

Timothée was born on the West Side of Manhattan in the colorfully named Hell's Kitchen (Clinton) district. Formerly a gritty, dangerous neighborhood overrun with gangs, guns, crime, and drugs, several legends compete to explain how Hell's Kitchen got its name. But there's no disputing why. From the mid-1800s into the 1980s, this Midtown area from 34th Street to 59th Street between Eighth Avenue and the Hudson River was one tough neighborhood.

During Prohibition, there were more speakeasies than children in the Irish Catholic area, run by gangsters like the rakish Owney "The Killer" Madden, who had a controlling stake in the Cotton Club in Harlem and associated with infamous Mafia boss Lucky Luciano. Following WWII, turf wars took place there between Puerto Rican immigrants and their Irish neighbors, a conflict romanticized in the musical *West Side Story* (1957).

The "gentleman gangster" Mickey Spillane ran the neighborhood like an Irish Godfather in the '60s and married into the local political dynasty, the McManus family. A war between Spillane and Jimmy Coonan, a younger rival, littered Hell's Kitchen with corpses from the late '60s until Spillane was shot dead in Queens in 1977, his murder an apparent mob hit.

Two generations of Irish gangsters, nicknamed the Westies by the police and the press, operated in Hell's Kitchen into the late '80s. Murder, theft, arson, extortion, gambling, loan-sharking, liquor, drugs, nightclubs—the Westies did it all.[4]

Gentrification from the '90s onward and the cleanup of neighboring Times Square transformed Hell's Kitchen, however, into what Mashable's Proma Khosla calls "the epicenter of aspirational New York…full of luxury high-rises, performance venues and exceptional restaurants, all located just a few minutes from the theater district and Times Square (if that's your thing)."⁵ Blocks of old tenements were demolished to make way for a growing forest of condominium towers. Dark bars became friendly bistros. Indeed, Hell's Kitchen is now more famous for television's chef Gordon Ramsay, whose series bears the area's name. The neighborhood is a mere shadow of what once inspired the creation of Marvel Comics' blind, super-powered, crime-fighting Daredevil.

For Timothée, his upbringing in the colorfully named, storied neighborhood was just the usual. He grew up in a 33rd-floor high-rise so close to the clouds that "it felt like we were literally floating in the sky" and rode the subway alone by age twelve.

A New Yorkman in France

Timothée's parents incorporated both Nicole's New York heritage and Marc's French heritage into their children's lives. During the year, Timothée lived in the States, but he summered overseas in the small town of Le Chambon-sur-Lignon, outside of Lyon, visiting his father's side of the family where they only spoke French. As stated, even while in the States, Marc only spoke to Timothée in his native tongue, which led to a bilingual lifestyle from a young age.

Timothée says all those summers in France were a big inspiration in his performance for *Call Me by Your Name*: "It's mostly time passing by without any pressure of the internet, the relationships, the showbiz."

He claims that he loved the small-town life; however, recovering from culture shock every time he would come back to his second home, or return to his current home, led to a cross-cultural identity issue. He remembers dreaming in French and in English, while constantly switching between his American cultural self and his French cultural self: "I became the French version of myself…impregnated with the culture."

He expounds on how he felt somewhat at a loss in his equilibrium in this cultural back and forth. "Oh, it led to an identity crisis, of sorts. I think it really helped with my acting," he says. "I'd be eight to nine months in Manhattan, then abscond for a few months to a small village in France." Despite the destabilization of it all, Timothée thinks the cultural dissociation helped him capture the essence of Elio in his breakout film, *Call Me by Your Name.*

"Your personality changes when you're using a second language," he mentioned in an interview with Matt Holyoak at *Shortlist.com.* "Certainly for me, my command of the language wasn't as strong [as my English], it doesn't come to me so easily…. [and] the way people carry themselves in France, compared to New York, I became a little more *deferential.* I would have to search a little more."[6]

Sports or Acting? Get that Acting Money

In fact, Timothée was so deferential to the French part of his cultural upbringing that, in his early years, he didn't want to be an actor at all. He became inspired by football (soccer). He still wanted to be in the limelight, just not the same limelight as his showbiz family. He dreamed of being a soccer star. He told *Verge* magazine in August 2017, "I coached six to ten-year-olds [at a soccer camp in France] when I was around thirteen. I was good at it, but the pay was not acting money."

When he came back to the States every year, he found himself bouncing between wanting to be a professional soccer player and a professional basketball player—acting truly wasn't even on his radar. He enjoyed playing on LaGuardia High School's basketball team alongside fellow actor Ansel Elgort, who, some years later, posted online from a Knicks game: "Laguardia high school pride. It's really crazy, Timmy and I played on the same basketball team, we had the same drama teacher Mr. Shifman, we had the same science teacher Mr. Singh, and then in the same year, both of us are nominated for a f$&king Golden Globe!!!"

The acting money wasn't always what he had hoped it would be though. When he was considering going to acting full-time, his mom pushed him to enroll at Columbia University instead. The diligent son, he acquiesced, but by the end of his freshman year, he was at the point where he just couldn't stay in school a moment longer—there was only one thing he could imagine doing with his life. Nicole begged him to stay put, but Timothée packed his things, left school, and moved to the Bronx where his family had been a couple generations before. He'd wrapped *Interstellar* by that time and "the idea of returning to the structured world of college felt stifling," he admits. Of course, he also told *GQ*'s Daniel Riley that he had hoped his role in *Interstellar* might be a little bigger, that it might serve as a breakout for him. When it didn't, a broke and disappointed Timothée Chalamet struggled in ways he had never expected.[7]

Lots of auditions followed, but no calls. He would watch movies that he'd read for and crouch down anxiously on the floor, rocking back and forth, feeling terrible. "I wanted to be *in* these films, not just watch them!"

One day, when Timothée felt the walls closing in on him, he found himself backstage in Montreal at a Kid Cudi show. He and Cudi, who Timothée calls one of his "musical heroes," hung out for a couple hours, and Cudi told Timothée about his own highs and lows. Cudi said you have to dig deep inside yourself and bring up a single-minded determination. Kid Cudi's advice stuck with Timothée, he even wrote much of it down and keeps it as notes on his phone. The takeaway? Cudi asked, "Are you, Timothée, the sort of person who can't possibly live any other way?"

Timothée nodded, getting it, feeling the determination bubbling up. "Fuck yeah."

Is He the Next Leonardo DiCaprio?

Trey Taylor with *Interview* magazine asks, "Is Timothée Chalamet the New Leonardo DiCaprio?"[8] Quite the claim considering Leonardo DiCaprio is known across the world for his countless leading roles and moving works. Does Chalamet stand up to such reverence? Is Chalamania, like Leomania of the late '90s, becoming a "thing?" Who is this Timothée Chalamet? And will he rise up to the occasion in the coming years as his still-blossoming career takes off?

Let's establish a little street cred for the lad, shall we?

Timothée Chalamet, whose name is technically pronounced "Timo-tay Shala-may"—his family calls him Timmy and friends call him Timothée or Timmy, as well— doesn't seem to care much what people call him. He'll answer to the French "ay" ending of his first name or the English "ee" ending. "Oh, whatever works," he once told movie critic Peter Howell of the *Toronto Star*. "It's supposed to be Timo-TAY, but that always seems like...too obnoxious."[9] Timo-TAY (or Timothée, *whatever*) was born in 1995 and has been featured in several works and films throughout his short time as an actor, yet his film presence is already enough that people are taking notice. Americans are always on the lookout for the next shining light in entertainment. In a short time, Timothée has placed himself center stage, the direct beam of the spotlight square upon his lean frame and wavy locks of dark hair and displaying his boyish grin.

In 2012, Timothée appeared in the second season of *Homeland* (2012), in which he played Finn Walden, the vice president's son. This led to his first major film role as the young version of Casey Affleck's character Tom in Christopher Nolan's *Interstellar* (2014), and then to arthouse-style, studio films like Jason Reitman's big-budget indie *Men, Women & Children* (2014) and *Miss Stevens* (2016). A role as Private Philippe DeJardin in Scott Cooper's must-see *Hostiles* (2017), a western starring Christian Bale, segued to Timothée's performances and more prominent roles in *Lady Bird* (2017) and *Call Me by Your Name* (2017).

"I think he's one of the best actors in the world…. Maybe he's the new Leonardo DiCaprio?" says *Call Me by Your Name's* producer, Rodrigo Teixeira. "He's a great actor, a great person, and he's given everything he has to do this film. We're so proud and happy to work with him."[10]

Akin to DiCaprio's breakthrough performance in *Titanic*, Luca Guadagnino's poignant coming-of-age drama *Call Me by Your Name* has had everyone raving about Timothée Chalamet. It garnered him his first Golden Globe nomination for Best Actor in a Motion Picture Drama and his first Academy Award nomination for Best Actor. The latter made Timothée the youngest actor, at age twenty-two, since 1939 to receive a Best Actor Oscar nomination and the third youngest ever—surpassed only by Mickey Rooney, who was nineteen in his 1939 performance in *Babes in Arms*, and by nine-year-old Jackie Cooper in 1930 for his performance in *Skippy*. Timothée's female counterpart amongst youngest nominees? Jennifer Lawrence, who also ranks third with her nomination at age twenty for *Winter's Bone*.

Of Timothée's performance in *CMBYN*, Daniel Riley wrote in *GQ*, "Every once in the rarest while, a young actor shows up in a movie *like an alien*—anonymous and yet in possession of such preternatural talent that audiences start thinking about the actor's future not in years but in decades. *Call Me by Your Name's* Timothée Chalamet is just such an alien and just such a once-in-a-generation talent."[11]

Another of Timothée's roles was in another film lauded in the 2018 awards season, *Lady Bird*, written and directed by Greta Gerwig. *Lady Bird* received an impressive forty-one nominations and thirteen wins. Among these were: Best Picture in the 2018 Academy Awards, Outstanding Directorial Achievement in Feature Film from the Directors Guild of America, and Outstanding Performance by a Cast in a Motion Picture from the Screen Actors Guild (SAG) Awards.

No small wonder Timothée has grabbed our attention. These achievements at his stage in the game are nothing short of astounding. Before 2017, Timothée had zero nominations or wins under his belt. Now that the nominations have started coming in, they may just never stop. The list of nominations goes on: Best Actor from the San Francisco Film Critics Circle; Breakthrough Performance from the Phoenix Film Critics Society; Best Lead Performance from the *Village Voice* Film Poll (he placed second); and numerous other "Best" nods.

Yet, those are his *nominations*. What about his *wins?* These include Most Promising Performer and Best Actor from the Chicago Film Critic Association, Breakout of the Year from the Indiana Film Journalist Association, Breakthrough Artist of the Year from the San Diego Film Critics Society, Actor of the Year from the London Film Critics' Circle, Best Performance of the Year (Actor) and the Rising Star Award from the Dorian Awards, and many other titles awarded to him just within a year.[12]

So clearly, this Chalamet kid has talent. Cred established.

EARLY ROLES

Molding the Raw Clay

Timothée's acting career began early, small bits in commercials and plays. According to an interview, he spent his first paycheck from a Disney commercial on Knicks season tickets when lots of New Yorkers were certain LeBron James was about to sign a deal. Of course, LeBron signed with the Miami Heat, so a disappointed Timothée often sprinted down to the Garden afterschool to scalp tickets and recover some of his Disney money.

He eventually broke into television, namely in four episodes of the USA Network's *Royal Pains* (2012) and in the recurring role of Finn Walden, troublemaking son of the vice president, on Showtime's *Homeland* (2012)—or, according to Timothée, "the asshole son"—wasn't that a song by Soundgarden?[1] The ball was rolling. He then landed film roles to play young versions of Casey Affleck and James Franco in *Interstellar* (2014) and *The Adderall Diaries* (2015), respectively.

---

[1] It was actually "Weird" Al Yankovic's magnificent takeoff of Soundgarden's "Black Hole Sun." (Chris Cornell, RIP.)

Meanwhile, Timothée attended New York's Fiorello H. LaGuardia High School of Music & Art and Performing Arts (the inspiration for *Fame*), following in his mom's and sister's footsteps, as well as those of Al Pacino, Jennifer Aniston, and Nicki Minaj. While there, he dated Madonna's daughter, Lourdes Leon, for almost a year. He got good grades and took acting seriously. According to a *GQ* interview, "…his first few years he couldn't crack the lead role in school musicals because that coveted spot belonged to an older big man on campus: Ansel Elgort."[13]

Amidst the wider film releases where he got to work alongside Matthew McConaughey and James Franco, Timothée also kept busy working on a few arthouse dramas and comedies: *Men, Women & Children* (2014), *One & Two* (2015), *Love the Coopers* (2015), and *Miss Stevens* (2016). All these roles in film and TV seemed to be molding the raw clay of what viewers would soon be presented with in his big breakouts in 2017.

One & Two was Timothée's first thriller. Directed by Andrew Droz Palermo, the film centers on a brother and sister discovering they have teleportation powers. Tender Zac (Timothée) and headstrong Eva (Kiernan Shipka) go to great lengths to keep their abusive father from discovering they are teleporting. *One & Two* is deeply suspenseful, depicting two teenagers fighting to feed their curiosities and explore who they are. "You see that it's genre-less," Timothée said of the film. "That's what really attracted me to this project. You have horror elements in there, you have action elements, you have superhero elements with the supernatural abilities. I'd love to do one of those franchise films, I would love to be jumping around. But it's exciting to do something that has elements of that but isn't that." *One & Two* is an enchant-ing glimpse at Timothée homing in on his signature acting qualities. There's his contemplative gaze, his slow, measured words, and his ability to simultaneously capture the angst and beauty of youth.

Love the Coopers follows the Cooper clan as four gen-erations of extended family come together for their annual Christmas Eve celebration. As the evening unfolds, a series of unexpected visitors and unlikely events turn the night upside down, leading them all toward a surprising rediscovery of family bonds and the spirit of the holiday. Timothée plays Charlie, a grandson in the throes of romantic infatuation, and although the film was largely panned as more tedious than tenderhearted, "Chalamet's talent as a passionate teen-ager is one of the highlights of this film. When he appears, any lull is dispelled and hope for the film's ability to entertain is ignited," according to film critic Carole Mallory.

In *Miss Stevens*, Timothée plays Billy, a rebellious teen-ager who gets taken under the wing of a caring teacher. The one place Billy can fully be himself is on stage. One of the greatest moments is when he stars in a production of *Death of a Salesman*, performing a powerful monologue that goes way beyond his years. It was the perfect moment for Timothée to put his fast-developing acting chops on full display. In an interview, he talks about how hard it was to slam-dunk the monologue. "Yeah, shooting that was like a marathon; we did maybe twenty takes of it," he says. "The first eight takes were good…and then maybe the four ones after that—there was really something. I think it's one of those that was used. And then maybe just eight extra. The monologue that plays in the movie—that was all in one take."

On crafting well-rounded characters, Timothée credits his experience working on *Homeland*. "When I watched it back, I always felt like there were moments where I just played the antagonist, as opposed to finding the real human in that," he told *Observer*.[14]

After filming *Interstellar*, he struck up a friendship with McConaughey, to whom he speaks on occasion for career guidance. "He [McConaughey] sees the roadmap for young male actors.... He's always tried to guide me in the right direction," Timothée says. "He embodies the idea that your career is a marathon, not a sprint. His career is so awe-inspiring. He navigated long periods for demand for honest and truthful acting."[15]

Filmography: Timothée Chalamet[2]

YEAR	TITLE	ROLE
2017	*Hot Summer Nights*	Daniel
2017	*Call Me by Your Name*	Elio Perlman
2017	*Lady Bird*	Kyle Scheible
2017	*Hostiles*	Pvt. Philippe DeJardin
2016	*Miss Stevens*	Billy
2015	*The Adderall Diaries*	Teenage Stephen
2015	*Love the Coopers*	Charlie
2015	*One & Two*	Zac
2014	*Interstellar*	Young Tom
2014	*Men, Women & Children*	Danny Vance

---

[2]   *Films only*

He admits, too, during this time it was difficult for him not to be a little starstruck by role models he'd meet either on set or during promotional events. In November 2017, Timothée found himself sitting next to Hugh Jackman and Jake Gyllenhaal at a *Los Angeles Times* roundtable discussion. "I've seen Hugh Jackman in a thousand Broadway shows," he said, lowering his voice so Jackman wouldn't overhear. "These are people I've been admiring for years, so it's hard not to feel differently around them. The rule I have for myself is that I try, at least, not to go, 'Oh my God! Oh my God!'"

BREAKOUT ROLES

The New Leonardo DiCaprio

Timothée Chalamet "is right smack dab in the middle of the hectic glow that is the minting of a Hollywood star," says The Village Voice's Alex Frank,[16] and *Interview* magazine tells us Timothée "has instigated a Chalamania akin to the Leomania of DiCaprio's late '90s apex." Further taking ownership of the phrase, the magazine goes on to say, "Chalamania was already taking hold after reviews out of Sundance Film Festival— where the film had its debut—began *worming* their way into the public consciousness."[17]

He has an adorability that prompted *Lady Bird* director Greta Gerwig to say jokingly, "They're gonna revive *Tiger Beat* just for him!" and Timothée's "a young Christian Bale crossed with a young Daniel Day-Lewis with a sprinkle of young Leonardo DiCaprio…raised speaking French in Manhattan and given a Mensa-level IQ and a love of hip-hop."

Timothée's trajectory does somewhat mirror that of a young Leonardo DiCaprio. Timothée Chalamet first appeared on TV series like *Royal Pains* and *Homeland* and in arthouse films like *Men, Women & Children* and *Miss Stevens*. This is much like how DiCaprio began in television. He landed roles on *Parenthood* and *Growing Pains*, followed quickly by indie films, *The Basketball Diaries* (1995), a biographical drama penned and based on troubled basketballer Jim Carroll, and then alongside Johnny Depp in *What's Eating Gilbert Grape* (1993) for which DiCaprio received an Oscar nomination at just nineteen.

So, after *Hostiles* and *Lady Bird*, along comes Timothée's *chef-d'oeuvre*, the critically acclaimed *Call Me by Your Name*, a love story that was nominated for six awards at the 2018 Independent Spirit Awards. Timothée won Best Male Lead for this breakout role. It's also where *CMBYN* producer Rodrigo Teixeira suggested Timothée is the "new Leonardo DiCaprio" and also said, "he's a great actor, a great person, and he's given everything he has to do this film."

MEL Magazine illustrates the comparison from their own perspective, stating, "While many gay films revolve around weighty topics like AIDS and prejudice, *Call Me by Your Name* is more like romance porn—this generation's gay *Titanic*."[18]

The Ringer's Andrew Gruttadaro feels likewise about the analogy, writing: "…the easiest comparison to make for Chalamet is Leonardo DiCaprio. Both actors came up on television; both were nominated for Oscars at young ages for their first true acting showcases…both bring their moms everywhere; both make questionable sweater choices; both probably vape."[19]

Hostiles

Hostiles premiered at the 2017 Telluride Film Festival and is a western set in the 1890s, starring Christian Bale as a hardened Army captain with a bloody past. It also features

Rosamund Pike, Wes Studi, Ben Foster, Jesse Plemons, and, of course, Timothée Chalamet.

Writer-director Scott Cooper, who is big on character motivation and backstory in his films, admits to *Backstage. com* that "the only actor who auditioned [for *Hostiles*] was Timmy Chalamet. I [had already] wrote the part for Christian Bale. I wrote the part for Wes Studi.... I generally tend to work with a rep company, or I just remember actors who never try to steal the scene, who never try to push an emotion. And Timmy, whose work I had never seen—he's a very uninhibited actor. He's not afraid to take risks. He has a really bright future."[20]

For such a young fellow, Timothée is both uninhibited yet discretionary and observant—a wonderful combination of traits. He appreciates watching his fellow actors on set, seeing every moment as a chance to study his trade. "I love being able to see how people sink into the material…watching [them] work [their] way through scenes, trying new things, always keeping it fresh. I got to work with Christian Bale over the summer, on *Hostiles*. It's so impressive.... I want to attack and to lead my life with vigor, but I'm in the watching stage at the moment. Younger actors feel pressure to bring a pop to every scene, as the roles get bigger—I'm finding you can add layers and do less scene-to-scene."[21]

Timothée admits he had multiple conversations with Bale while filming *Hostiles* and would grill him about *American Psycho* and *Dark Knight*, trying to glean whatever he could to apply to his own work. He also admits he wanted to know the secret on how Bale is so prolific yet still manages to keep his private life private.

Regarding the film itself, the reception has been mixed yet mostly positive. *RogerEbert.com* reviewer Godfrey Cheshire awarded it three stars and said, "The film has a lot going for it. Besides the gorgeous, burnished look supplied by cinematographer Masanobu Takayanagi, Cooper gets a range of fine performances from a topnotch cast," and goes on to name several cast members, including Timothée. *Rolling Stone* calls it a "powder keg of a western" and "a film whose brute force [is] tempered with contemplative grace…a potent and prodigious achievement." The *Chicago Tribune*'s film critic Michael Phillips calls it "a solemnly bloody tale of white redemption in the Old West" and specifically mentions Timothée as the "Young Actor of the Moment." *The Portland Mercury* dubs *Hostiles* a "grim, regret-filled, mud-covered, symbolism-laden tale" and calls attention to "newly minted 'it' boy Timothée Chalamet as a slender, French-accented private who's not quite sure why he was chosen for the mission."

So *Hostiles* has turned out to be quite a feather in Chalamet's cap, even if his role is marginal. It was a great learning experience and just the beginning of his meteoric 2017, our young actor of the moment is off and galloping towards great things.

Lady Bird

Greta Gerwig's debut as a solo director, *Lady Bird*, debuted at the 2017 Telluride Film Festival and stars Saoirse Ronan as restless high school senior Christine—who is nicknamed Lady Bird. Gerwig mined her own Sacramento adolescence to write the film, which has the sharpness and specificity of lived experience. It's a winsome bit of autobiography that rings with bittersweet truth and acutely captures the heady blur of the last year of high school when old things gradually matter less and less as new opportunities and excitements tantalizingly tease on the horizon.[22]

Gerwig admits to discovering Timothée Chalamet through one of her friends. The self-proclaimed "theater nerd" told a panel after a SAG screening of the film, "he was in a play in New York that I was pointed to…. It's my favorite way to watch actors because there is nothing intervening with me watching them work. There is something about actors who are used to a stage—it gives them the space to act with their wholes [sic] bodies."[23] She further admits this is one of her favorites methods of discovering up-and-comers.

After seeing him on stage, Gerwig got in touch with Timothée and—long story short—offered him the role of Kyle Scheible in *Lady Bird*, a character who stoically breaks the heart of Saoirse Ronan's titular protagonist. Timothée says he felt challenged by the role, that he wanted to bring some humanity to the character. "It was important for me that I didn't just sit as an antagonist…. Hopefully people… see that character as an antagonist that is genuinely suffering, has real emotions, and is living a sad existence," he admitted, and was also quick to over-defensively point out to Jimmy Fallon on *The Tonight Show* with hands raised: "Hey, I am nothing like that character!"

In *Lady Bird*, Timothée's shaggy-haired, wealthy teen spends most of his time either paranoid about the world or focusing on his rock band. Timothée says on prepping for his *Lady Bird* role, "She [Greta] gave me a book called *The Internet Does Not Exist* and said, 'This is what your character would be reading.' It's like long-winded, formulaic equations on why the Internet requires everyone to be on the grid, with a lot of Y2K theory. I opened it up and there was a bunch of manic scribbling everywhere in the book and I thought, 'Oh my god, Greta, what thrift shop did you get this at? Whoever was reading this before you was really going through some serious paranoid stuff!' And she said, 'Those are all my notes!'"

Timothée remembers thinking then about Greta, *Jesus, you're not Lady Bird, you're Kyle!*

He admits it with a laugh, of course, and fully embraced the role of the anarchist teenager. One fan described Kyle as "a total asshole, unlikeable player until he meets a girl, Athena Rose.... But will he allow his reputation to be ruined to be with this girl? Or will he break her heart just like the many, many girls that came before her?" Another fan on Tumblr admits Kyle is "a total douchebag but just proves Timmy can play any role!!!"

Obsev.com honors Timothée's character in *Lady Bird* as one of the "2017 Movie Characters We Loved to Hate," saying, "If you didn't date a Kyle Scheible in high school, you *were* a Kyle Scheible in high school. Timothée Chalamet (who had a hell of a year) imbues this pretentious weasel with the perfect mix of white male entitlement and adolescent ignorance. But when Lady Bird falls for him, we totally get it."[24]

Jimmy Kimmel asked in an interview, "Are you friendly with him? Timothée Chalamet? You guys were also, he was in *Lady Bird*, as well."

Saoirse blushingly replied, "Yeah, we smooched a lot."

Still, Timothée is nothing like Kyle, else Saoirse and he wouldn't be seen happily chumming around with each other at the various film awards, giggling arm-in-arm and swapping awards for photoshoots at the Annual Palm Springs

International Film Festival, rocking similar edgy black ensembles at the 75th Golden Globe Awards or commiserating at the 2018 SAG Awards red carpet interview about how people butcher their names. "Saoirse is great," he says, giving her an 'I'm-not-worthy' bow, making her giggle. "I saw Saoirse in *Brooklyn* and thought she was the most incredible actress and that was one of the big reasons I wanted to jump into *Lady Bird*. She inspires me to work extra hard."

The two seem to have struck up a true friendship on set. In fact, in a recent interview with Ellen DeGeneres, Saoirse said, "You know even if it's just a platonic relationship I think Timmy and I have a nice companionship together. What I mean, like, we're very compatible as companions."

At the Santa Barbara International Film Festival, Timothée looked adoringly down from behind the podium at Saoirse. "I thought to myself, I want you to think I'm cool. Saoirse, listen, I wanted you to think I was cool...," his voice cracked with emotion before continuing, "because *you* are so fucking cool."

Saoirse charged the stage and hugged him. "I'm just going to take Timmy home," she announced. "He's my prize."

Timothée reflected later to IMDB at the Globes, expressing his incredulity, appreciation, and admiration for the ladies of *Lady Bird*. "I'm fresh out of drama school. I was hitting audition rooms five years ago for TV shows that now I feel like they're difficult for me to watch [because he didn't get the coveted parts]. It's like, you know, with Greta and Saoirse, these women are geniuses! I don't know how I found my way into a mother-daughter romance of the ages. I'm very fortunate."

Call Me by Your Name

Well before any of *Interview* magazine's christening of this so-called *Chalamania* incursion, filmmaker Luca Guadagnino had been trying for a few years to produce *Call Me by Your Name*, an adaptation of the 2007 coming-of-age novel by André Aciman—a book that has become like a canon for LGBTQ readers.

A tranquil, sun-dappled, speculative film set in the cobbled streets and cool waters of northern Italy in 1983, *CMBYN* is all about exploration, life, connection, summer, and really nice Ralph Lauren shirts. It became the darling of the 2017 indie festival circuit, raking in commendations for everything from its stirring and sensitive portrayal of love and futility to its softly redolent soundtrack by artist Sufjan Stevens.

Where did Timothée come in? Guadagnino found him through Brian Swardstrom, an agent who had just signed the young actor. "We met, and it was instant recognition," Guadagnino recalls. "I had lunch with Timothée for the first time [and] I immediately saw in his physicality the kind of feverish, nervous angularity that André described in the book…most important, in conversation with Timothée, I learned that the young man was not only a veteran actor, having acted for many years already in TV, theater, and even cinema, but he had the most intoxicating ambition to be a *great* actor."[25]

Something about Timothée's presence during that lunch with the filmmaker hit home. "…[he] had a brooding, unbiased determination and…and yet he had this kind of soft, ingénue naiveté of a young boy. Those two things together were incredible." By the time they had finished their con- versation, Guadagnino was convinced Chalamet *was* the embodiment of Aciman's Elio Perlman. He auditioned no one else after that meeting, giving Timothée the role. "I just saw an incredibly articulate, bright, smart, artistically ambitious young man, someone who not only had a sense of self that was completely un-narcissistic but had ambition to make sure his art as an actor was shining on-screen,"[26] Guadagnino said.

As some folks know—and many more may not—it took almost three years for filming to begin as James Ivory's treat- ment of André Aciman's 2007 novel as an intellectual romance had a difficult time gaining traction with studios due to its material, "…taking forensic apparatus to unpick male desire with a new, frank and often breath-taking immersion…" and containing erotic scenes between two men, as well as that in which "Chalamet conducts with a peach that will likely cause future blushes on the fruit and veg aisle of Sainsbury's for everyone who sees it. The film luxuriates in its sexuality in detail."[27]

But once Luca Guadagnino went "all in" with Ivory, things were underway.

Call Me by Your Name is a love story in its most unadul- terated form. Elio is the seventeen-year-old boy whose narra- tion guides us in Aciman's novel, as he meets Oliver (played by Armie Hammer), a twenty-four-year-old graduate student come to stay for the summer at Elio's father's Italian villa. To embody the role of Elio, Timothée came on location in Crema, Italy, five weeks early. He arrived speaking fluent French, of course, but he had to train at speaking Italian and playing piano and guitar, and he spent four hours daily in his lessons. Even though he was bilingual, "Learning the Italian was tough," Timothée told *Newsweek* in an interview. "I tried to really come at from a purist perspective, really learn the grammar, syntax and conjugations. And I'm proud of the job I do with the Italian in the movie, but I would maybe just do it phonetically if I had to go back and do it again."[28]

Timothée's speaking French wasn't always part of the role; it isn't in Aciman's novel. Guadagnino and screenwriter James Ivory decided to reshape Elio's character a bit, fashioning it around Timothée: "...the great Bernardo Bertolucci said: 'When you shoot a movie, you must leave a door open to reality,'" stated Guadagnino. "Timmy is half American and half French, and we implemented this part of his essence. We made sure we could really use his *Frenchness*...[his] multilingual personality and also *his* [own] personality."[29]

Though Chalamet shared love scenes with three different screen partners—Hammer, Esther Garrel, and, as fans of the novel know well, a peach—the actor is quick to brush off any awkwardness around these encounters. Or tries to, explaining on *Jimmy Kimmel Live!*, yes, there *is* a peach in the story and sometimes "one must explore, as one does." He then goes on to beg Kimmel to "please don't roast me, please don't make a peach joke," with hands pressed together in prayer, knowing Kimmel is set to host the 90th Oscars.

"I'm worried that fifty years from now I'll be signing peaches from behind a desk," he says, laughing, then mimicking like he is indifferently signing and, with a world-weary gaze, handing the autographed fruit to people.

Kimmel laughs. "That's your vision of hell."

But Timothée knows when to joke and when to treat the message seriously. "There is no evil antagonist in this film or

Timothée Chalamet

villain. It's just a real story with human fluctuations of love, which requires emotional honesty," he said in an interview with *Vanity Fair*. "Armie [Hammer] and I decided before the movie started that was going to be the biggest challenge.... It wasn't the sexual parts, but the idea that the entire soul of the film is between these two men."[30]

There are those who point to Guadagnino's knowledge of movies, saying he rivals Quentin Tarantino for the ease with which he can relate subjects to cinema. He told *Deadline Hollywood* he sought Armie Hammer for the part of Oliver, waxing lyrical about how good he is in Gore Verbinski's *The Lone Ranger*, in spite of its challenging critical reception. "It's a beautiful movie," he insists; in it, he felt Hammer had the movie star quality that the Oliver of Elio's wistful glance needed to encapsulate. "But also, there is a sensitivity to him that is so deep."[31]

A sensitivity that both Armie and Timothée share, and which easily allowed friendship to bud between them. They both arrived early, hung out in Crema, and talked excitedly about the project. "[There] was a proximity our souls felt to one another in those early weeks," Timothée recalls. "The friendship sprouted very easily, very naturally, very organically. It was really the random luck of the universe."[32]

When they reunited on the press trail months later, Armie told journalists, "I was video Skyping with Timmy last night. It feels like I got a new best friend and brother out of the process. There was a huge amount of trust we put in one another to do this. It required a level of vulnerability in both of us that would only have been possible if we felt safe around each other, and we did."[33]

Filmography: Armie Hammer[3]

Year	Title	Role
2006	*Flicka*	Male prefect
2008	*Blackout*	Tommy
2008	*Billy: The Early Years*	Billy Graham
2009	*Spring Breakdown*	Beachcomber boy
2009	*2081*	Harrison Bergeron
2010	*The Social Network*	Cameron and Tyler Winklevoss
2011	*J. Edgar*	Clyde Tolson
2012	*Mirror Mirror*	Prince Andrew Alcott
2012	*The Polar Bears*	Zook
2013	*The Lone Ranger*	John Reid / The Lone Ranger
2015	*Entourage*	Himself
2015	*The Man from U.N.C.L.E.*	Illya Kuryakin
2016	*The Birth of a Nation*	Samuel Turner
2016	*Nocturnal Animals*	Hutton Morrow
2016	*Free Fire*	Ord
2016	*Mine*	Mike Stevens
2017	*Call Me by Your Name*	Oliver
2017	*Final Portrait*	James Lord
2017	*Cars 3*	Jackson Storm
2018	*Sorry to Bother You*	Steve Lift

---

[3] *Films only*

TIMOTHÉE'S PERSONALITY

Timothée Chalamet is referred to as a "slip of a thing" and has a sharp and enthusiastic presence with a performer's instinct on how to fill a room, according to *GQ*, which also says Timothée "has [an] antic energy, a rubber-ball bounciness. He has the body of a kid raised in New York, stovepiped like a Stroke, the sort of frame that's forged in high schools without football teams. He's taller than he comes off in *Call Me by Your Name* (at six feet, he's dwarfed on-screen by co-star Armie Hammer's five extra inches) and has an angular face that looks to require shaving once or twice a year."

"Let me tell you something," Armie says to Ode Entertainment's Melissa Nathoo. "In *Call Me by Your Name* there's an adjustment period for houseguests, right? I'll tell you what kind of houseguest Timothée is. Timothée will be sitting on your couch and he'll be eating pistachios and all a sudden he'll look down and realize he has a handful of pistachio shells and go, 'Oh, I'll just tuck these in between the couch cushions here—'"

Timothée grins but protests, "That is not entirely true—"

"That IS entirely true," Armie interrupts with a laugh.

"No, I pride myself on my politeness as a guest and, in fact, there's no part of my life that I'm stronger in," all of this said with a facetious grin, while Armie folds his arms and shakes his head at Nathoo.

"Seriously," Timothée says, "you always have the best pistachios."

"Yeah, I can tell you enjoy them because I always find the shells everywhere."

Are we seeing the rise of film and TV's new *Odd Couple*, perhaps?

"Seriously, though," Armie says when asked about his impression of Timothée, "one of my favorite things about him is the sort of unguarded openness he brings and the rich internal life he wears right on the surface, and he lets everybody in to that; that's also what makes him such a phenomenal actor and makes his performances so incredible."

"Oh, I just adored working with him," says Saoirse Ronan, *Lady Bird*. "He's lovely and kind and very brilliant at acting. A brilliant actor. And I love his hair, his lovely hair." No mention of pistachios by Ronan.

Timothée is still so new to the scene, there's not an ounce of jadedness in him. He seems to get a kick out of meeting celebrities, or what he refers to as the "titans of my age." He excitedly told Jimmy Kimmel he couldn't believe he was coming on his show following Oprah Winfrey.

"You met Oprah backstage?" Kimmel asked.

Timothée rubs his hands together. "I did, I did," he gushed, "and she has the softest hands in the world. And she said my name in 'the' voice!"

"Oh yeah," Kimmel said. "The Oprah 'voice.' 'Timothée Chalamaaaaaay!' She said she was really excited to meet you."

You can tell it's surreal to the young man, the limelight. Very much a 'pinch-me-I-must-be-dreaming' change of pace from the acting stage or sleepy Crema, Italy. Indeed, during the annual Oscars luncheon in early February 2018 at the Beverly Hilton, he found himself rubbing elbows with A-listers and Hollywood royalty, taking selfies with Steven Spielberg, Meryl Streep, Guillermo del Toro, Kobe Bryant, and Academy governor Laura Dern. He marveled to Jimmy Fallon on *The Tonight Show* that he met Angelina Jolie and Jennifer Aniston in rapid succession at the Golden Globes and "was like, 'Oh my god! Which side are we on?'" He reflects again on the various occasions where, "I look out in the room and it's like all these actors and directors I've admired for a long time and my mouth is moving and I'm like, 'Oh my God, they're listening to me right now!' It's really surreal. It is so strange. It doesn't make sense."

Joaquin is Number One for Me

Frank Ocean: "You've worked with a lot of legends already. Who's your all-time favorite actor?"
Timothée Chalamet: *"Dude, Joaquin Phoenix.... There's five or six artists I'm really trying to follow in the footsteps of creatively. I get the opportunity to be on the phone with one right now [laughs], but on the acting side, Joaquin is number one for me."*

He confesses, "I'm a simple guy. I'm a plain cheese pizza kind of guy. I mean, I might add sausage maybe? But I'm not going to wade into the pineapple debate.... I just have an openness to life and the universe. Hobnobbing with famous people? That's crazy."

Nineteen-year-old Chalamet fan Kelechi Alfred-Igbokwe gave her take in *The Wellesley News*: "Chalamet's personality is so appealing...because he is so genuine. He's humble, at times bashful, sometimes awkward, often deliriously smiley, but always honest, without appearing overly refined or polished. He also has the infectious quality of being intellectual without being pretentious, which is a breath of fresh air in Hollywood. He has a deep appreciation for film-making and often cites wisdom he has gained from studying past great actors."

In a *Variety* "Actors on Actors" segment, fellow thespian and first-time Best Actor nominee Daniel Kaluuya (*Get Out, Black Panther*) got together with Timothée for a one-on-one interview. Regarding their meeting, Timothée talked later about how much he enjoyed it and told *Vanity Fair*, "*Get Out* is one of my favorite movies of the year and Daniel has been the one person that I can consistently look at, lock eyes with, and ask, 'What the fuck is happening right now?' Because these are totally surreal environments to be in [regarding the nominations and all the buzz]."

Kaluuya went on to ask Timothée in the *Variety* get-together about working with Luca, curious about how the director works: "So, in terms of him [Luca] not auditioning people, how was that meeting, then? What do you feel like he was trying to see out of you?"

Timothée responded, "I have this impression with other people I meet with sometimes—I'm curious if you have it too—they're just, like, *sussing* you out, and they're feeling out your vibe, which is weird, because you don't want to be fake...certainly there's a level of artificiality to all of this, but, you wanna be real. When else do you eat with someone and they're just like, judging you, you know? Making assumptions about you."

"That would be called a 'date,'" said Kaluuya.

"Oh, yeah! Right." Timothée doesn't particularly like that word: *date*. He calls it scary. "Date is very much a scary word," he told *GQ*, "because then that context has been established. You can always see people on early date behavior."

Vogue magazine has likened his moments to "nothing short of a light in the darkness," dubbing him their 2018 awards season "obsession," saying they love Chalamet "because he is all of us."[34] His enthusiasm and star-stricken mannerisms reflect how we, as fans or cinephiles, might acquit ourselves if suddenly and unexpectedly discovering the red carpet beneath our feet and flashbulbs in our eyes.

Yet this starry, dewy-eyed approach is an intrinsic part of Timothée's appeal and character. It captures us, this kind of earnest receptivity and friendliness in which he engages with anyone, is excited to talk to anyone about anything but especially movies and acting. He brings a certain skittish energy into the room with his soft gaze, frequently and abashedly scanning the floor as he smiles in genuine happiness and appreciation just to be in anyone's presence and a chagrined thankfulness when paid compliments of any sort.

"This feels so not a given," he admits with sincere humility. "And I worry that the bubble may suddenly burst. The fact that mainstream media and television is giving the independent films I've been in any kind of love, I am just thankful, so thankful."

Independent or not, Oscar nominations are most certainly mainstream, Timmy.

Even he cannot deny his celebrity is rising—as self-effacing as he might be, typically deflecting attention onto his directors, co-stars, interviewers, or anyone but himself. However, it is his work that excites him most, that drives him forward, and he never tires of talking about film and acting and supporting causes dear to him, all of which can only happen from the work he puts into his career. "Ultimately, the goal is to focus on the work," he says. "To create the best art, to make something that is fresh and relevant and important. I realized: the platform I have exists because of the work. With the work comes more opportunities. But those opportunities bring a sense of responsibility, too. It was just important to me, as someone young, coming into this industry, to do something good."

CRITICAL RECEPTION

Call Me by Your Name

Call Me by Your Name landed four Oscar nods for Best Picture, Best Adapted Screenplay, Best Original Song, and Best Actor for Timothée Chalamet. The Palm Springs International Film Festival presented Timothée with the Rising Star Award, as well: "Timothée Chalamet gives a stirring performance as Elio, a seventeen-year-old on the brink of passion and self-discovery [in *Call Me by Your Name*]," festival chairman Harold Matzner said in a statement. "It's an intimate and erotic performance that transports the audience to another time and place and stays with us long after we've left the theater."

The film is unquestionably good. It has a 93 on Metacritic[35] (second among current releases, behind *Lady Bird*) and has been critically lauded. *Slate*'s Dana Stevens echoes Matzner's statement: "Some of its images…stay with you afterward like memories of your own half-remembered romance."

When asked about how he connected with the character of Elio, Timothée talked of how he started by absorbing the source material—Aciman's novel and James Ivory's screenplay adaptation of it—and how he thought about how it reminded him of Stephen Chobsky's *The Perks of Being a Wallflower*. There's something "unabashed" yet "accurate" about both films, he says. He talks of how he appreciated the way *Call Me by Your Name* is "such an intimate lens into the random mania of a young person's desire and inhibitions." He adds, "There's a tension on the surface of [Elio's] existence…he's in a transitionary period in his life, becoming a man and dealing with feelings of sexual impulse for the first time. It felt rare to read a story about a young person this complex. It's no surface representation of what young people are…. As an actor, you *seize* that kind of opportunity."[36]

Rarely does an interview go by that Timothée isn't asked about when the character is exploring his sexuality, such as when a sex scene with a certain fruit (the illustrious peach scene) takes place. Armie Hammer joked in an interview they did together with Josh Horowitz of MTV News that every fifteen or twenty years there needs to be a rehash of the *American Pie* scene (*Vogue* magazine calls it "the highbrow answer to Jason Biggs's pie sex of yesteryear"). Timothée is able to chuckle about it, but when asked to elaborate, he said, "…as an actor you always look to your director to kind of gauge what mood they're in, what and how they're doing and such, and I just saw how that day Luca wasn't treating that scene with any ceremony. He just treated it like any other day, so by the time we got around to shooting it just felt like any other scene with dialogue or a breakfast scene. It just felt like anything else. If Luca had treated it differently, maybe I would have been shaking. [But] it didn't feel salacious or exploitative. Those sensual moments in the film served the love story."

Regarding the Oscar nomination, Timothée says humbly, "The experience of getting to shoot it was the main appeal….

The reception it's been getting is above and beyond our wildest dreams, anything beyond that would be greatly appreciated too, but I'm really trying not to think about that too much." In another interview, he stated, "I went for a huge film two years ago that I didn't get and I was devastated for about six months. I'm not being hyperbolic. So, I'm pinching myself now, that aside from academic evaluations of the film, having seen people viscerally react to [*CMBYN*] at Sundance and Berlin, whether because they're reminded of an experience, or they wish they'd had that experience, what it's already been has been more than I could've ever asked for."

Armie Hammer, his co-star in the film, minces less on Timothée's Oscar-worthy performance: "Timothée is so fucking good in this movie. Having seen him go into this project and then watch him as a person rise to the occasion in such a magnificent way and then turn in a performance that is so stellar, I feel lucky to have gotten to witness the whole process."[37]

Timothée remarks in one interview, prior to the film's release, "Some people in journalism saw [*Call Me by Your Name*], like, a year ago. And at some of these fancier parties, actors I've been looking up to and studying for years have seen it. But for those who the movie was made for, and for my buddies at home, they still haven't seen it!" When pressed further on who the movie was made for, Timothée thought a moment then said, "…young guys, particularly Americans, because I feel the mental health dialogue is less repressed in Europe the way it is here, will see this movie and see there's nothing wrong with being themselves. There's nothing wrong with opening up and playing your cards. In fact, sometimes it can be an attractive and beautiful thing."[38]

Yes, there is certainly a cross-generational contention in *CMBYN* that ruffles feathers—to Timothée it feels parenthetical. He, Luca, and Armie discussed it, and they emphatically agreed that as Elio and Oliver's attraction intensified throughout the film, all the moralistic arguments became *"weightless.* We felt very comfortable with the film," says Luca Guadagnino, who is openly gay and has come under fire somewhat from LGBTQ communities for casting straight actors (i.e., Timothée and Armie). He told *The Hollywood Reporter*, "I couldn't have ever thought of casting with any sort of gender agenda. I think people are so beautiful and complex as creatures that as much as I am fascinated with gender theory...I prefer much more never to investigate or label my performers in any way."[39]

So as far as any negative reaction to the context, they have largely dismissed it.

It's about an emotional journey. "Butterflies in the stomach is the most beautiful feeling you can feel, no?" Luca says, then points further to Timothée's soft, "ingénue naiveté of a young boy."

Ira Madison III, an openly gay black man, appreciated the film for what it was, telling Condé Nast: "What I loved about [the film] was...it stripped away, for the most part, the heterosexual gaze. I think it's much easier to watch on the second or third viewing...because gay audiences aren't trained to watch a movie like that and not expect something awful to happen.... If you watch it again...you're able to enjoy it without any of the bullshit of an HIV scare, homophobia, or a disapproving parent. None of that is gonna happen."

A gay eighteen-year-old named Luke tells *MEL Magazine* being able to connect with other *Call Me by Your Name* fans has given him a sense of community he's never had before. "We're all in love with [Timothée]," he says. To Luke and many other young LGBTQs, Chalamet represents a new breed of celebrity. "It's so refreshing to see a straight male in the spotlight who doesn't feel the need to constantly reinforce his masculinity," Luke says.[40]

Armie Hammer commented to the British *GQ* on *CMBYN* and the topic of masculinity: "I never think about masculinity.... For the first time, you see a movie with two men, who feel something for each other and decide [to]... discover this new place in a sweet, tender way, and there is no wife at home, no conflict, no-one getting sick.... You just see two men be sweet and tender with each other. Which catches people off-guard."

The LGBTQ Entertainment Critics Association felt similarly. GALECA (previously known as the Gay and Lesbian Entertainment Critics Association) announced *Call Me by Your Name* topped the winner's list of its annual Dorian Awards, honoring the film overall in five total categories, including Film of the Year and LGBTQ Film of the Year. Timothée was twice recognized; for his performance as Elio, and with the 'We're Wilde About You!' Rising Star Award.

And for those in the LGBTQ community who still take exception to the role of straight actors playing gay characters, Julia Elia Leschi of the *Washington Times Square*, NYU's independent student newspaper, says it best: "The notion that, in order to believably act out a love story between two men, one needs to have experienced such love in real life undermines the very concept of acting...in the same way gay actors can believably play the role of a straight person, like Ellen Page did in *Juno* and *Whip It*."[41] Page, after coming out in 2014, seems to have suddenly been pigeonholed, of course, proving the Hollywood perception of the LGBTQ community still has a way to go.

Julia's closing paragraph in her op-ed:

In our own Tisch School of the Arts, students are preparing to take on the world of entertainment. Future gay actors should not be caged into any roles, and future gay directors and writers should produce the stories that matter to them with the knowledge that the casting is truly open. Chalamet and Hammer's performances in *Call Me by Your Name* were admirable. If you still want to boycott *Call Me by Your Name*, don't do it because of the casting.[42]

LOOKING TO
THE FUTURE

That Acting Money

The year 2017 made a real difference for Timothée.

For one thing, he finally come into that acting money. Chalamet stressed that the first dream as an actor was "economic sustainability," with the critical acclaim coming a close second. "Every actor dreams of being economically sustainable," he insists. "I worked with John Goodman on a movie, and he said he felt like he'd made it when he could sustain himself."

He admits, "[I left college because] I had this feeling I couldn't *not* act and, yet, to get there I really needed teachers…to make me comfortable with failing. To be bad and get over it—that opened the floodgates. I did a play in New York when I was fifteen, after this really difficult but ultimately helpful sophomore year in high school; that's when it kind of took off for me. I'm also passionate about music. I want to pursue other things creatively, not so much music, but definitely writing and directing. I'm going to be very, very patient about that. The dream as an actor is to be economically self-sustainable and what this year has been is beyond that now. I'm getting a creative license of sorts."[43]

At the 2018 Santa Barbara Film Festival, Saoirse Ronan spoke about Timothée, saying, "I'm so proud of you, I'm so proud of the work that you've done in our film [*Lady Bird*] and in *Call Me by Your Name* and everything that you're gonna do." The crowd interrupted her with a cheer. "Yeah, he's brilliant, and he's got a good head screwed on his shoulders, and I'm very, very proud to know him."

When posited the question on increases in his paycheck since his Oscar nomination, Timothée laughs it off and applies his customary unquiet modesty. "It reminds me of that scene in *Birdman*, 'I'm just waiting for someone to tell me I've made it.'"[44]

It seems rather clear when one is nominated for an Oscar for a best leading role in a film in their very *first* leading role ever, they're well on their way.

Stovepiped like a Stroke? Be a Berluti Model

With a preference for slim-cut suiting in quirky colors, Timothée Chalamet has a talent for choosing the coolest looks straight off the catwalk. Superlative acting chops aside, Timothée's waiflike six-foot tall "It" Boy frame (he's taller than he looks—in *CMBYN*, he's often standing beside Armie Hammer, who happens to be 6' 5") and fashion sensibilities has attracted other perks, chiefly notice in the fashion industry.

"[Being involved] with fashion has been really fun, just as a fan. I've been following designers like Raf, Haider Ackermann, Hedi Slimane—these guys are like rock stars. They're artists."

—Timothée Chalamet

Shortly after making this statement, of course, Haider Ackermann, the Creative Director of Berluti at the time, ended up designing Timothée's all-white Oscars tuxedo—because, according to *Thrillist.com*, "he is the purest human at the Oscars." The upshot of being a muse for a fashion label? You get to wear their clothes for free. It's not "acting money," but Ackermann was sending Timothée all kinds of sweet threads before exiting Berluti, and we have a feeling he's received several packages from Gucci, Calvin Klein, Adidas, and Warby Parker as well.

The Wellesley News's Kelechi Alfred-Igbokwe says, "The icing on the cake…is Chalamet's fashion sense. He is the king of quirky, creative style and has become known for wearing artful sweaters with unique designs to press events. I love a guy with good taste!" Timothée's fashion sense has even inspired fan websites such as chalametstyle on Tumblr. Give it a look.[4]

Hot Summer Nights

A coming-of-age thriller from A24 studios and DirecTV, *Hot Summer Nights* is set during the summer season on Cape Cod and centers on a shy out-of-towner named Daniel, played by Timothée Chalamet, who is coping with his dad's death by being transplanted to Cape Cod for the summer. He gets in way over his head after he begins selling weed for the neighborhood drug dealer. At the same time, he sparks a romance with the drug dealer's sister, who burns a little brighter than everyone else in town (played by Maika Monroe, whom he is

---

[4]   https://chalametstyle.tumblr.com

rumored to have dated briefly during filming), which starts a fast-paced triangle of love and betrayal. The film evokes everything from *Rushmore* and *The Virgin Suicides* to *The Sandlot* and *Goodfellas*, taking viewers back to 1991, when America was trying to grow up without letting go of its glory days.

The writer and director, Elijah Bynum, wanted Timothée from the beginning. "We knew him mostly from *Homeland*, and then *Interstellar* came out right as we were starting to cast. Ryan [Friedkin, the producer] was like, 'Timothée is Daniel,' so he had that role basically from day one…unfortunately, we tortured him a little bit and stretched out [the casting process] for four months, but he was always it. His trajectory from awkward goofy boy to drug runner is a pretty big arc to try and do believably, and he did a great job with that."

"Weed is a central part of the film," Timothée explains about *Hot Summer Nights*. "It's more accessible now obviously, but in the time period that's one of the central themes to the movie, because it takes place in 1992 in Cape Cod, it was a felony drug offense. That's a big catalyst [in the film], because you have this weird legal mess that's conflicting Daniel while he also has these relationships that are falling apart, whether it's with best friends or intimate people in his life."

The character, Daniel, is certainly conflicted with being a good person or a rebel. When asked about his rebellious nature, Timothée laughed. "Elijah [Bynum] is more of the rebel, you know?" he told ET Canada. "At twenty-eight years old, he wrote an incredible script that was a throwback to a time that he didn't actually live in—he was one year old in 1992." And when asked about how the cast got along, he pointed out, "We all lived together in one house in Atlanta and it was a lot of fun. We all got along well. We're all rather young, so there wasn't a generational gap like on some film sets. Everybody came together, and there was a certain relatability amongst us all. We all went through a similar process."

He and Maika Monroe struck up some chemistry in the film, and she admitted they got along great in person. She joked to Young Hollywood that she and her other *Hot Summer Nights* co-stars called Timothée 'Timo' (tee-mo), and he was perfectly fine with it.

"Call me whatever," he often admits to interviewers, perhaps a tad bit already over being asked how to pronounce his name for millionth time. (Keep winning awards and that question will go away eventually, Timothée!)

Hot Summer Nights is Chalamet's first release since earning his Oscar nomination for *Call Me by Your Name* and, according to *IndieWire* "seems to fit nicely into the company's [A24's] growing slate of visually distinct coming-of-age stories, from *Spring Breakers* to *Lady Bird*."

Beautiful Boy

Amazon Studios debuted the first footage from its upcoming awards contender *Beautiful Boy* at CinemaCon, and the first reactions are overwhelmingly positive. Press in attendance called the brief footage "devastating" and "harrowing" and the film a "potential awards powerhouse."[45]

An April 26, 2018, a tweet by *Hollywood Life* contributor Avery Thompson stated, "I just watched an emotionally charged scene from #BeautifulBoy with Timothée Chalamet & Steve Carell. This movie is going to emotionally destroy me. Also, just go ahead & give Timmy the Oscar. It's going to be hard for anyone to top him. #CinemaCon."

The film is adapted from David Sheff's biographical book *Beautiful Boy: A Father's Journey Through His Son's Addiction*, which recounts the author's struggle watching his son, Nic, fall into methamphetamine addiction. Nic Sheff later authored *Tweak: Growing Up on Methamphetamines*, published by Simon & Schuster and featured on *Oprah.com*. In it, Nic states he was drunk for the first time at age eleven and, in the years that followed, he would regularly smoke pot, do cocaine and Ecstasy, and develop addictions to crystal meth and heroin.

Steve Carell plays David Sheff in the movie, while Timothée plays his son, Nic. *IndieWire* says, "The role is expected to bring Chalamet back into the awards conversation less than a year after 'Call Me by Your Name' earned him his first Oscar nomination."

"I've never given myself more to any project in my life," Timothée said. "I lost twenty pounds to do it because I'm playing a methamphetamine addict. I got to work with Steve Carell for two or three months. Similar to *Call Me by Your Name*, we really gave it everything, we laid it all on the line. It's a really powerful and moving memoir."

At CinemaCon, Carell said, "The movie tries to depict [that with issues like addiction]…there are no easy answers. It's not presented like the cinematic version of this problem or this relationship. It felt very true to me and very real."

A bad audio connection via Skype kept the crowd from hearing Chalamet's response. "Rest assured that whatever he just said was incredibly articulate," assured Carell, who called his onscreen son "one of the most profound young people I've ever met."

Beautiful Boy Author's Dedication

"I was like every parent I know. We think this can never happen to our family—to our beautiful girls and beautiful boys. But I learned the hard way that no family is immune—anyone can become addicted. When it happens to someone we love, we think we're alone, but we aren't. There are millions of us.... *Beautiful Boy* is dedicated to those who suffer the disease of addiction and those who love them. And it's dedicated to those we've lost because of this disease. Sharing our stories about whatever we struggle with isn't a panacea, but openness is the beginning of healing. You aren't alone."

—David Sheff

At the time of this publication, *Beautiful Boy* is slated to open in select theaters October 12, 2018. The film marks the English-language debut of Belgian director Felix Van Groeningen, best known for *The Broken Circle Breakdown*, and co-stars Maura Tierney, Amy Ryan, and Timothy Hutton. We have no doubt Timothée will be walking the red carpet for it soon enough, during next awards season.

A Rainy Day in New York
(a.k.a. the Woody Allen Effect)

According to a press release, *A Rainy Day in New York* suggests the film will depict some college seniors over the course of a rainy weekend—not a day, despite the title. Those students are characters played by Timothée, Selena Gomez (whom Timothée is rumored to have dated in 2018—"We're just friends," he has said. The fact they were romantic on screen may have confused people into thinking they are more than friends in real life), and Elle Fanning, who become involved in some sort of love triangle.

Still, it seems whatever good things to come out of the performances in *A Rainy Day in New York* will be marred by the attachment of writer-director Woody Allen, of which this would be his forty-eighth feature film. Several numbers shy of this, with his film career just taking off, Timothée has already been forced to navigate some tricky waters.

He was initially excited by his work on *A Rainy Day in New York*, calling it "…an awesome working experience, being able to tell a New York story in the tradition of *Manhattan* or *Annie Hall*…. And to be opposite Elle Fanning and Selena Gomez and Jude Law for a month and a half is quite a humbling experience," yet the backlash of working with Woody Allen came quickly upon the heels of the not-yet-released film's production. Timothée's humbling experiences and meteoric rise have come during a time when Hollywood has been flipped on its back and had its underbelly exposed. Allegations of long-hidden abuses, misogyny, and sexual misconduct by those in power are numerous indeed.

Allen was accused in 1993 of abusing his adoptive daughter, Dylan Farrow, as a child (courts found there was not enough evidence at the time to support Dylan's accusations). The subject of an open letter penned by Farrow in 2014 for *The New York Times* has reignited debate about Allen's role in Hollywood.[46] Farrow followed this in 2017 with another op-ed in the *Los Angeles Times* questioning why the #MeToo movement—which has terminated the careers of alleged predators like Harvey Weinstein—has spared Woody Allen, calling on actresses like Greta Gerwig (who acted in *To Rome with Love* with Allen, nominated for best director for *Lady Bird*) and Kate Winslet to denounce the man.[47]

Though Gerwig felt conflicted for some time, she has joined the list of actors listed by *The Washington Post* who now refuse to work with Allen; among them: Colin Firth, Rachel Brosnahan, Ellen Page, Susan Sarandon, Jessica Chastain, Mira Sorvino, David Krumholtz, and now, Timothée Chalamet.[48] The #MeToo and #TimesUp revolutions have penetrated every sector of the entertainment industry, and one of the hot topics following renewed accusations by Dylan Farrow are against Woody Allen. And, ultimately, Timothée took a stance alongside those distancing themselves from the writer-director, although it must be pointed out he did not escape the pains of a few uneasy interview questions, through which he maneuvered not without some awkwardness expected of a young person tackled with sudden and sharp criticism.

Like his fellow actors Selena Gomez, Elle Fanning, Rebecca Hall, and Griffin Newman on *A Rainy Day in New York*, Timothée officially declared he was donating the money he earns from the movie. Newman made his decision public just a few days after *The New York Times* ran its first explosive report about Weinstein. Newman posted on Twitter in October 2017:

> "I need to get this off my chest:
> - I worked on Woody Allen's next movie.
> - I believe he is guilty.
> - I donated my entire salary to RAINN."

Timothée chose Instagram as his vehicle of choice, stating he will split the funds among the Time's Up Legal Defense Fund, the LGBT Center in New York, and RAINN (Rape, Abuse & Incest National Network), the largest anti-sexual violence organization in the United States.

The post has over a quarter of a million Facebook "likes," and here are his own words:

"This year has changed the way I see and feel about so many things; it has been a thrilling and, at times, enlightening education. I have, to this point, chosen projects from the perspective of a young actor trying to walk in the footsteps of more seasoned actors I admire. But I am learning that a good role isn't the only criteria for accepting a job—that has become much clearer to me in the past few months, having witnessed the birth of a powerful movement intent on ending injustice, inequality and, above all, silence.

I have been asked in a few recent interviews about my decision to work on a film with Woody Allen last summer. I'm not able to answer the question directly because of contractual obligations. But what I can say is this: I don't want to profit from my work on the film, and to that end, I am going to donate my entire salary to three charities: TIME'S

UP, The L.G.B.T. Center in New York, and RAINN. I want to be worthy of standing shoulder to shoulder with the brave artists who are fighting for all people to be treated with the respect and dignity they deserve."

Timothée states he was inspired to donate his salary after seeing the wave of activism that has taken over Hollywood, that he simply didn't want to profit from his work on the film, and went on record to say he believes Allen is guilty of the claims against him by his adopted daughter—all of which place him in the good graces of millennial audiences, who have high expectations of social consciousness from the film stars of their generation.

Perhaps Hollywood may be beginning to feel the same way? The *New York Post*'s "Page Six" reported in January 2018:[49]

> The sun may be setting on "A Rainy Day in New York" — before the Woody Allen movie ever even sees the light of day.
>
> Sources tell The Post that the film, which is due to be distributed by Amazon later this year, may not make it to the screen.
>
> "'Rainy Day' will either not come out or [will] get dumped by Amazon without any p.r. or theatrical release," said one film-industry executive.

And:

> Insiders predict that, even if "A Rainy Day in New York" ever sees the light of

day, none of its actors will even support their own work.

"There will be no premiere, no print or TV ads, no interviews. No one will promote it," said a movie distribution executive.

"I wonder if it will even make Cannes?" speculated a film festival insider of the May event. "The French love him and don't care about sex scandals. But Amazon does. Jeff Bezos is not dumb."

Yet another more recent post, dated May 8, 2018, states:[50]

Allen is still working on the film's post production. Page Six also appears to confirm the film will be released by Amazon, who has a deal with Allen at the moment.

The way Timothée has comported himself at this time makes him even more evocative. In fact, he has risked being vocal when men three times his age are still silent. Though he has taken the high road, citing contractual obligations prevent him from elaborating much more, he will say that supporting good causes [for him] can only happen from the work he's put into his career thus far. "Ultimately, the goal is to focus on the work," Timothée posted online. "To create the best art, to make something that is fresh and relevant and important. I realized: the platform I have exists because of the work. With the work comes more opportunities. But those opportunities bring a sense of responsibility, too. It was just important to me, as someone young, coming into this industry, to do something good."

Timothée's statements reflect the candor, honesty, and grit we are already coming to expect from the sensitive and intelligent young actor. In respect to the #MeToo movement, "I feel very lucky to have an older sister [Pauline] who always pointed out the dynamics of what it's like when a woman shares her ideas, how they're received compared to men's ideas. And being young, hopefully getting to act for years on end, changing that is our responsibility now—and our good fortune."[51]

Being forthright and standing for what's morally right and against inequality and prejudice are important platforms for him. On his Instagram account, he wrote: "I want to be worthy of standing shoulder to shoulder with the brave artists who are fighting for all people to be treated with the respect and dignity they deserve."

Some Films You Do for the Studio, Some You Do for You

Timothée's been in quite a few independent roles now, which he claims is more by chance than design, but he appreciates it. Asked if he'd do something like a *Transformers* flick: "…hey, as Kanye put it, Guillermo del Toro made *Pacific Rim* and that's one of his favorite movies. His latest movie, *The Shape of Water*, is amazing. Christopher Nolan is tied with Paul Thomas Anderson [as] my favorite director. If one of those auteurs has a two-hundred-million-dollar film and wants me to be a part of it, fuck yeah." Personally, we believe Chalamet would make a cool Nightwing. Are you listening, DC Comics?

The King

Another future role for Timothée includes the lead in David Michôd's Netflix epic *The King*, in which he'll play King Henry V. The film follows Henry V after his brother is killed in battle just before his coronation. The death forces young Henry to rise to the occasion and lead England against a potential war with France. The movie marks Michôd's second Netflix movie following the Brad Pitt-starring *War Machine*. Pitt's production company, Plan B, is producing *The King*. Actor Joel Edgerton co-wrote the script with David Michôd. *Vanity Fair* says, "*The King* has all the trappings of a solid prestige picture with awards-season potential."

Greta Gerwig Eyes Little Women with Meryl Streep, Saoirse Ronan, Timothée Chalamet

According to *Variety*: "Following her critically acclaimed and Oscar-nominated *Lady Bird*, Greta Gerwig is eyeing *Little Women* as her next directing gig. A-listers Meryl Streep, Emma Stone, Saoirse Ronan, and Timothée Chalamet are in talks to star in Columbia Pictures' retelling of the American classic. The movie would mark a reunion for Gerwig, Ronan, and Chalamet—the young actors starred in 2017's coming-of-age comedy, *Lady Bird*."

Photo Gallery

Above: Armie Hammer and Timothée Chalamet at the
2017 Berlin International Film Festival.

Above: Timothée Chalamet at the 2018 Tortonto Film Festival.

Below: Timothée Chalamet signs a peach for a fan at the 2018 Toronto Film Festival.

Above: The cast of *Call Me By Your Name* at the 2017 Berlin International Film Festival.

Above: Timothée Chalamet at the 2014 Toronto Film Festival.

TIMOTHÉE ON ACTING

In a Film4 interview, Leonardo DiCaprio talked about what inspires and drives him. "Being an actor is the first thing I remember wanting to do in life. I remember at fourteen, fifteen years old spending months and months watching all the great classic films, all the great performers of the past, and being so incredibly inspired by them and saying, 'one day I want to come close to doing something that good'…so I think that thirst or that drive to just achieve what I believe is something as good as those heroes, that's what continues to make me want to do this."

It's a quote we could just as easily hear attributed to Timothée.

When asked what it's like to play such contrasting characters as Kyle in *Lady Bird* and Elio in *Call Me by Your Name*, Timothée says, "That's what you dream of as an actor, and I'm lucky to have such great roles so early on. Elio particularly is more sympathetic on the page and his instincts and behaviors are more understandable, yet it's also fun to take on a character like Kyle when a lot of the audience is repulsed by him but he's very much a human character at the same time."

71

To Daniel Kaluuya in "Actors on Actors," Timothée reveals some of his own doubts in trusting his instincts. "Something I struggle with," he says, "and I struggled with this even when I was in drama high school, is you have your instincts, but then you think to yourself, 'What, I'm twenty-one or younger. What do I know?' But what's nice now is I'm learning to trust my instincts, and I'm reading things more."

He took some of Daniel's advice to heart too—to read scripts "for fun," analyze them and identify what he likes as an actor in the script. "[I read them] so then, I'm more informed in why I wanna say no to something or I wanna say yes to something," Daniel said. "A lot of the time it's just about knowing thyself."

"That's so cool. I'm stealing that," Timothée responded rubbing his hands together, inspired from sitting across from his fellow actor and award nominee. Both actors come across as open-minded people who looking to learn from those around them no matter who they are, a great attribute to have in any young actor, actress, or filmmaker.

In the discussion of reading and saying yes or no to scripts, Timothée elaborated on why he chose *Lady Bird*. "It was not just the role, but who I got to work with—like, Greta and Saoirse and getting to work with them. With Greta, I had seen *Frances Ha*, and then just reading [the *Lady Bird*] script she wrote, it was so specific, and everything was so detailed, which is what I like about the movie, because they're relatable, 'normal' characters, yet everything is so specific. One of my favorite lines I have in the movie is 'I haven't lied in two years,' which is like 'who speaks like that?' Like he was keeping track, so pretentious!"

CONCLUSION

Timothée guesses he's made it now since he's starting to get recognized. He left a restaurant the other day, and someone was suddenly in his face taking photos, snapping shots off like wildfire and following him down the sidewalk.

"Ah, you're getting hounded by pushy gangs of paparazzi now?" asked Jimmy Fallon in a *Tonight Show* interview.

"Well, one," Timothée clarified.

"Oh, one?"

"Yeah, just one guy. One paparazzi."

They both laugh.

A similar conversation took place with Neil Patrick Harris when he hosted *Jimmy Kimmel Live*:

> "You're getting recognized a lot when you go out now?"
>
> Timothée looked simultaneously abashed and excited. "The other day I got paparazzi'd for the first time."
>
> "Paparazzi'd?" Neil Patrick asked. "It's a verb?"
>
> "Isn't that how you say it when it happens?"

"Normally. What did it feel like?"

"I was shocked. I don't know, it was super weird. You're coming out of a restaurant or whatever, then all of a sudden someone's at you, and it's as if you've done something terribly wrong."

"They're all snapping pictures," Neil Patrick emphasized, obviously having had dozens of run-ins over the years of his own career. "It's very aggressive."

"Well, there was, like, *one guy.*" Timothée shifted in his seat, perhaps feeling like he needed to deflect the attention. "He probably thought I was Freddy Highmore or something."

Neil Patrick paused a beat. "You're better looking than Freddie Highmore."

Timothée turned bright red and hid his face, crouching forward in his seat. "You can't say that on TV!"

"I'm the host, and I just did."

No offense to Freddie Highmore, who made an adorable Charlie Bucket before he became a disaffected Norman Bates (and admits they get mistaken for each other, and also that he loves *Call Me by Your Name*), but more than just Neil Patrick Harris agrees Timothée is quite a catch. Enter Marta Pozzan—a globe-trotting model who goes from fashion week to fashion week advertising brands from Kenzo to Bulgari and beyond—who was revealed as Timothée's "mystery blonde" makeout partner during last year's Cannes Film Festival;

their "getting acquainted" activities made "Page Six" head-lines. Evidently, they had been introduced to each other that very night by singer Abel Tesfaye (The Weeknd), and their hook-up made news by the following day. "The Cut" called it "a very Leo DiCaprio move to make out with a twenty-some-thing model at Cannes." Perhaps Timothée is underselling it a bit stating he's been pursued by a solitary paparazzo?

When asked, "What do you wanna do now? What do you aspire to next?"

Timothée replied:

> "Things have been going very well for me, so I don't know. I guess I feel like I have to suffocate the moment with apprecia-tion or something sometimes, really sit in it, and it's tough because—I don't know, not tough, these are great things—I'm just navigating a new space, all these new things. That's what it feels like.
>
> "And I watch things I did when I was nineteen and I go, 'Man, I'm so thankful that I have two years [more experience] now on that.' I just know I'm going to watch things four, five years from now and go, 'oh, man, I was clueless,' or, God forbid, I'm like 'those were the glory years!'"

He laughed and slumped in his chair. "And now I'm all washed up. But, yeah, I just wanna work." He darts back up. "Just keep working and keep looking for good directors, good projects, and important storytelling—that's the goal for me, to keep doing things like that."

So, maybe he didn't win an Oscar for *Call Me by Your Name*. That's okay. He was a dark horse in the race despite the all-white Berluti suit. The main thing is his nomination was more like a celebration, a parade in honor of the Year of Timothée.

Thrillist.com said it best: "He conquered Hollywood when he conquered America's heart this winter. The Oscar is merely a footnote."

Timothée is just twenty-two at the time of this biographical work. As you know by now, he's all about learning from the legends, he's remaining humble. And he's having a ball!

Timothée isn't going anywhere—Matthew McConaughey promised.

Chalamania has only just begun.

<u>Lesser Known Facts About Timothée Chalamet</u>
- Favorite food: Any kind of bagel with cream cheese.
- Favorite toys as a kid: Power Rangers.
- Favorite Halloween costume: "I went one year as Yu-Gi-Oh, which is in the same ecosystem as Pokémon, and I had an incredible haircut and cool necklace. I was also Broadway Spider-Man on crutches one year."
- Favorite pet: Urtle the Turtle ("still my pet")
- Favorite rap name: Little Timmy Timothée
- Favorite birthday: "I don't have one because my birthday is December 27, so I end up hoarding my gifts after Christmas."
- Favorite celebrity crush: Judi Dench
- Favorite first album: 50 Cent's *Get Rich or Die Tryin'*
- Favorite social media: Mostly active on Twitter (@RealChalamet) and Instagram (@tchalamet)

Timothée's Awards

A full listing showing all thirty-three wins and forty-three nominations to date of this publication.[52]

Academy Awards, USA

2018	**Nominee** Oscar	Best Performance by an Actor in a Leading Role *Call Me by Your Name* (2017)

Golden Globes, USA

2018	**Nominee** Golden Globe	Best Performance by an Actor in a Motion Picture - Drama *Call Me by Your Name* (2017)

BAFTA Awards

2018	**Nominee** BAFTA Film Award	Best Leading Actor *Call Me by Your Name* (2017)
	Nominee EE Rising Star Award	

AACTA International Awards

2018	**Nominee** AACTA International Award	Best Lead Actor *Call Me by Your Name* (2017)

Alliance of Women Film Journalists

2018	**Nominee** AWFJ EDA Award	Best Actor *Call Me by Your Name* (2017)

Austin Film Critics Association

2017	**Winner** Austin Film Critics Award	Best Actor *Call Me by Your Name* (2017)
	Winner Breakthrough Artist Award	*Call Me by Your Name* (2017) *Lady Bird* (2017) *Hostiles* (2017)

Awards Circuit Community Awards

2017	wWinner ACCA	Best Actor in a Leading Role *Call Me by Your Name* (2017)
		Best Cast Ensemble *Lady Bird* (2017) Shared with: Saoirse Ronan Laurie Metcalf Tracy Letts Lucas Hedges Beanie Feldstein Lois Smith Stephen Henderson Odeya Rush Jordan Rodrigues Marielle Scott
	Nominee ACCA	Best Cast Ensemble *Call Me by Your Name* (2017) Shared with: Armie Hammer Michael Stuhlbarg Amira Casar Esther Garrel

Boston Online Film Critics Association

| 2017 | Winner BOFCA Award | Best Actor *Call Me by Your Name* (2017) |

Boston Society of Film Critics Awards

| 2017 | Nominee BSFC Award | Best Actor *Call Me by Your Name* (2017) |

Broadcast Film Critics Association Awards

2018	**Nominee** Critics Choice Award	Best Actor *Call Me by Your Name* (2017)

Central Ohio Film Critics Association

2018	**Nominee** COFCA Award	Best Actor *Call Me by Your Name* (2017)
		Actor of the Year *Call Me by Your Name* (2017) *Hostiles* (2017) *Lady Bird* (2017)
		Breakthrough Film Artist (for acting) *Call Me by Your Name* (2017) *Hostiles* (2017) *Lady Bird* (2017)

Chicago Film Critics Association Awards

2017	**Winner** CFCA Award	Best Actor *Call Me by Your Name* (2017)
		Most Promising Performer *Call Me by Your Name* (2017)

Chicago Independent Film Critics Circle Awards

2017	**Nominee** CIFCC Award	Best Actor *Call Me by Your Name* (2017)

Chlotrudis Awards

2018	**Winner** Chlotrudis Award	Best Actor *Call Me by Your Name* (2017)

Dallas-Fort Worth Film Critics Association Awards

2017	**Nominee** DFWFCA Award	Best Actor *Call Me by Your Name* (2017) 4th place

Denver Film Critics Society

2018	**Nominee** DFCS Award	Best Actor *Call Me by Your Name* (2017)

Detroit Film Critics Society, US

2017	**Nominee** DFCS Award	Best Actor *Call Me by Your Name* (2017)
		Breakthrough Artist *Call Me by Your Name* (2017) *Hot Summer Nights* (2017) *Lady Bird* (2017)

Empire Awards, UK

2018	**Nominee** Empire Award	Best Male Newcomer *Call Me by Your Name* (2017)

Film Independent Spirit Awards

2018	**Winner** Independent Spirit Award	Best Male Lead *Call Me by Your Name* (2017)

Florida Film Critics Circle Awards

2017	**Winner** FFCC Award	Best Actor *Call Me by Your Name* (2017)
	Winner Pauline Kael Breakout Award	

Gay and Lesbian Entertainment Critics Association (GALE-CA)

2018	**Winner** Dorian Award	Film Performance of the Year - Actor *Call Me by Your Name* (2017)
		We're Wilde About You! Rising Star of the Year

Georgia Film Critics Association (GAFCA)

2018	**Nominee** GAFCA Award	Best Actor *Call Me by Your Name* (2017)
	Nominee Breakthrough Award	*Call Me by Your Name* (2017) *Hostiles* (2017) *Hot Summer Nights* (2017) *Lady Bird* (2017)

Gold Derby Awards

2018	**Winner** Gold Derby Award	Lead Actor *Call Me by Your Name* (2017)
		Breakthrough Performer
	Nominee Gold Derby Award	Ensemble Cast *Call Me by Your Name* (2017) Shared with: Vanda Capriolo Amira Casar Victoire Du Bois Esther Garrel Armie Hammer Michael Stuhlbarg
		Ensemble Cast *Lady Bird* (2017) Shared with: Beanie Feldstein Lucas Hedges Stephen Henderson Tracy Letts Laurie Metcalf Jordan Rodrigues Saoirse Ronan Odeya Rush Marielle Scott Lois Smith

Golden Schmoes Awards

| 2017 | **Nominee** Golden Schmoes | Breakthrough Performance of the Year *Call Me by Your Name* (2017) |

Gotham Awards

2017	**Winner** Gotham Independent Film Award	Breakthrough Actor *Call Me by Your Name* (2017)

Hamptons International Film Festival

2017	**Winner** Variety 10 Actors to Watch	

Hollywood Film Awards

2017	**Winner** Hollywood Breakthrough Award	Breakthrough Actor *Call Me by Your Name* (2017)

Houston Film Critics Society Awards

2018	**Nominee** HFCS Award	Best Actor *Call Me by Your Name* (2017)

Indiana Film Journalists Association, US

2017	**Winner** IFJA Award	Breakout of the Year *Call Me by Your Name* (2017) *Lady Bird* (2017)

Indiewire Critics' Poll

2017	**Winner** ICP Award	Best Lead Actor *Call Me by Your Name* (2017)

International Cinephile Society Awards

2018	**Winner** ICS Award	Best Actor *Call Me by Your Name* (2017)

International Online Cinema Awards (INOCA)

2018	**Winner** INOCA	Best Actor *Call Me by Your Name* (2017)

Iowa Film Critics Awards

2018	**Nominee** IFC Award	Best Actor *Call Me by Your Name* (2017)

Kansas City Film Critics Circle Awards

2017	**Winner** KCFCC Award	Best Actor *Call Me by Your Name* (2017)

London Critics Circle Film Awards

2018	**Winner** ALFS Award	Actor of the Year *Call Me by Your Name* (2017)

Los Angeles Film Critics Association Awards

2017	**Winner** LAFCA Award	Best Actor *Call Me by Your Name* (2017)

MTV Movie & TV Awards

2018	**Nominee** MTV Movie + TV Award	Best Performance in a Movie *Call Me by Your Name* (2017)

National Board of Review, USA

2017	**Winner** NBR Award	Breakthrough Performance *Call Me by Your Name* (2017)

National Society of Film Critics Awards, USA

2018	**Nominee** NSFC Award	Best Actor *Call Me by Your Name* (2017)

New York Film Critics Circle Awards

2017	**Winner** NYFCC Award	Best Actor *Call Me by Your Name* (2017)

New York Film Critics, Online

2017	**Winner** NYFCO Award	Breakthrough Performance *Call Me by Your Name* (2017)

North Carolina Film Critics Association

2018	**Nominee** NCFCA Award	Best Actor *Call Me by Your Name* (2017)

Online Film & Television Association

2018	**Winner** OFTA Film Award	Best Breakthrough Performance: Male *Call Me by Your Name* (2017)
	Nominee OFTA Film Award	Best Actor *Call Me by Your Name* (2017)
		Best Ensemble *Lady Bird* (2017) Shared with: Saoirse Ronan Laurie Metcalf Tracy Letts Lucas Hedges Beanie Feldstein Lois Smith Stephen Henderson Odeya Rush Jordan Rodrigues Marielle Scott

Online Film Critics Society Awards

2017	**Winner** OFCS Award	Best Breakthrough Performance *Call Me by Your Name* (2017)
	Nominee OFCS Award	Best Actor *Call Me by Your Name* (2017)

Palm Springs International Film Festival

| 2018 | **Winner**
 Rising Star Award - Actor | *Call Me by Your Name* (2017) |

Phoenix Critics Circle

| 2017 | **Winner**
 PCC Award | Best Actor
 Call Me by Your Name (2017) |

Phoenix Film Critics Society Awards

| 2017 | **Nominee**
 PFCS Award | Breakthrough Performance
 Call Me by Your Name (2017) |

San Diego Film Critics Society Awards

| 2017 | **Winner**
 SDFCS Award | Breakthrough Artist |
| | **Nominee**
 SDFCS Award | Best Actor
 Call Me by Your Name (2017) |

San Francisco Film Critics Circle

| 2017 | **Nominee**
 SFFCC Award | Best Actor
 Call Me by Your Name (2017) |

Screen Actors Guild Awards

2018	**Nominee** Actor	Outstanding Performance by a Cast in a Motion Picture *Lady Bird* (2017) Shared with: Beanie Feldstein Lucas Hedges Tracy Letts Stephen Henderson Laurie Metcalf Jordan Rodrigues Saoirse Ronan Odeya Rush Marielle Scott Lois Smith
		Outstanding Performance by a Male Actor in a Leading Role *Call Me by Your Name* (2017)
2013	**Nominee** Actor	Outstanding Performance by an Ensemble in a Drama Series *Homeland* (2011) Shared with: Morena Baccarin Claire Danes Rupert Friend David Harewood Diego Klattenhoff Damian Lewis David Marciano Navid Negahban Jackson Pace Mandy Patinkin Zuleikha Robinson Morgan Saylor Jamey Sheridan Hrach Titizian

Toronto Film Critics Association Awards

2017	**Nominee** TFCA Award	Best Actor *Call Me by Your Name* (2017)

Vancouver Film Critics Circle

2017	**Nominee** VFCC Award	Best Actor *Call Me by Your Name* (2017)

Village Voice Film Poll

2017	**Nominee** VVFP Award	Best Lead Performance *Call Me by Your Name* (2017) 2nd place

Washington DC Area Film Critics Association Awards

2017	**Nominee** WAFCA Award	Best Actor *Call Me by Your Name* (2017)

Women Film Critics Circle Awards

2017	**Nominee** WFCC Award	Best Actor *Call Me by Your Name* (2017)

Young Entertainer Awards

2016	**Nominee** Young Entertainer Award	Best Young Ensemble Cast - Feature Film *Love the Coopers* (2015) Shared with: Blake Baumgartner Maxwell Simkins

ENDNOTES

1   "Weather History for New York JFK, NY | Weather Underground." n.d. Accessed May 13, 2018. https://www.wunderground.com/history/airport/KJFK/1995/12/27/WeeklyHistory.htm.

2   The Corcoran Group. n.d. "Corcoran, Nicole Flender, West Side 888 Seventh Avenue Realtor, Real Estate Agent, Broker, Referral, Experience, New York, Manhattan, Brooklyn." The Corcoran Group. Accessed May 15, 2018. https://www.corcoran.com/nyc-real-estate/agents/west-side/nicole-flender/13691.

3   Flender, Harold. 1963. *Rescue in Denmark*. New York: Holocaust Library.

4   Strausbaugh, John. 2007. "Hell's Kitchen - New York City - Weekend Explorer." *The New York Times*, August 17, 2007. https://www.nytimes.com/2007/08/17/arts/17hell.html.

5   Khosla, Proma. 2016. "What If 'Daredevil' Took Place in the Real Hell's Kitchen?" *Mashable*. March 19, 2016. https://mashable.com/2016/03/19/daredevil-hells-kitchen-irl/.

6   Mandle, Chris. 2018. "Timothée Chalamet on Grappling with Rebellion, Addiction and Speaking

out." *ShortList*. February 21, 2018. https://www.short-list.com/entertainment/films/timothee-chalamet-inter-view-rebellion-addiction-speaking-out/346503.

7   Riley, "…Right on Time."

8   Taylor, Trey. 2018. "Is Timothée Chalamet the New Leonardo DiCaprio?" *Interview*. April 5, 2018. https://www.interviewmagazine.com/film/timothee-chalamet-new-leonardo-dicaprio.

9   Howell, Peter. 2017. "Rising Star Timothée Chalamet Talks Sex Scenes, His Mother and More." *The Toronto Star*, December 14, 2017. https://www.thestar.com/entertainment/movies/2017/12/14/rising-star-timo-the-chalamet-talks-sex-scenes-his-mother-and-more.html.

10   "'Call Me By Your Name' Producer Labels Timothée Chalamet The 'New Leonardo DiCaprio.'" 2018. *Esquire*. March 5, 2018. https://www.esquire.com/uk/culture/a19081974/call-me-by-your-name-produc-er-labels-timothee-chalamet-the-new-leonardo-dicap-rio/.

11   Riley, Daniel, and Ryan McGinley. 2018. "Timothée Chalamet Has Arrived Right on Time." *GQ*. February 14, 2018. https://www.gq.com/story/timothee-chalamet-has-arrived.

12   "List of Awards and Nominations Received by Timothée Chalamet." n.d. Accessed May 16, 2018. https://en.wikipedia.org/wiki/List_of_awards_and_nomina-tions_received_by_Timoth%C3%A9e_Chalamet.

13   Ibid.

14   Zahn, Paul. 2018. "Breakout Star Timotheé Chalamet on How His 'Homeland' Role Influenced 'Lady

Bird.'" *Observer*. January 22, 2018. http://observer.com/2018/01/timothee-chalamet-says-home-land-role-helped-prepare-for-lady-bird/.

[15] Mandle, Chris. 2018. "...Rebellion, Addiction and Speaking out."

[16] Frank, Alex, Aaron Gordon, Joshunda Sanders, Lara Zarum, Bilge Ebiri, Jake Offenhartz, and Emma Whitford. n.d. "Timothée Chalamet's New York State of Mind." Accessed May 16, 2018. https://www.villagevoice.com/2018/01/12/timothee-chalamets-new-york-state-of-mind/.

[17] Taylor, "...the New Leonardo DiCaprio?"

[18] Blum, Steven. 2018. "The Queer Kids Who Can't Get Over 'Call Me by Your Name.'" *MEL Magazine*. January 9, 2018. https://melmagazine.com/the-queer-kids-who-cant-get-over-call-me-by-your-name-d967b-c764dca.

[19] Gruttadaro, Andrew. 2018. "Timothée Chalamet Losing at the Oscars Is a Good Thing." The Ringer. *The Ringer*. March 5, 2018. https://www.theringer.com/movies/2018/3/5/17080766/timothee-chalamet-oscars-best-actor-leonardo-dicaprio.

[20] "Why Oscar Nominee Timothée Chalamet Was the Only Actor Who Auditioned for 'Hostiles.'" 2018. *Backstage.com*. January 23, 2018. https://www.back-stage.com/interview/why-oscar-nominee-timoth-ee-chalamet-was-only-actor-who-auditioned-hostiles/.

[21] McConaughey, Matthew. 2017. "Timothée Chalamet" *Interview*. June 2, 2017. https://www.interviewmaga-zine.com/film/timothee-chalamet.

22 Lawson, Richard. 2017. "Saoirse Ronan Shines in Greta Gerwig's Deeply Personal Directorial Debut." HWD. *Vanity Fair.* September 2, 2017. https://www.vanityfair.com/hollywood/2017/09/lady-bird-greta-gerwig-review.

23 Zahn, "Breakout Star Timotheé Chalamet…"

24 Smith, Greg. 2017. "2017 Movie Characters We Loved To Hate." *Obsev.* December 18, 2017. https://www.obsev.com/galleries/2017-movie-characters-loved-hate/655887.

25 Riley, "…Right on Time."

26 Miller, Julie. 2017. "Inside Timothée Chalamet's Overnight Breakout." HWD. *Vanity Fair.* December 5, 2017. https://www.vanityfair.com/hollywood/2017/12/timothee-chalamet-call-me-by-your-name-breakout-star.

27 Flynn, Paul. n.d. "Timothée Chalamet and Armie Hammer on Friendship, the Oscars and That Peach Scene." British *GQ.* Accessed May 26, 2018. http://www.gq-magazine.co.uk/article/armie-hammer-timothee-chalamet-interview.

28 Menta, Anna. 2017. "Timothée Chalamet on 'Call Me By Your Name,' Vulnerability and That Peach Scene." *Newsweek.* November 24, 2017. http://www.newsweek.com/2017/12/29/timothee-chalamet-interview-call-me-your-name-720407.html.

29 Riley, "…Right on Time."

30 Miller, "…Chalamet's Overnight Breakout."

31 Utichi, Joe. 2017. "Luca Guadagnino And Cast On 'Call Me By Your Name' And The Alchemy Of Conjuring The Butterflies Of First Desire." *Deadline.*

November 15, 2017. http://deadline.com/2017/11/
call-me-by-your-name-armie-hammer-timothee-chala-
met-oscars-interview-1202207499/.

32   Ibid.

33   Ibid.

34   Ruiz, Michelle. 2018. "Timothée Chalamet Is Officially
2018's Awards Season Obsession." *Vogue*. January 11,
2018. https://www.vogue.com/article/timothee-chala-
met-oscars-golden-globes-awards-season-obsession.

35   *Call Me by Your Name*. 2017. Sony Pictures Classics.
http://www.metacritic.com/movie/call-me-by-your-name.

36   Utichi, "…Butterflies Of First Desire."

37   Flynn, "Timothée Chalamet and Armie Hammer on
Friendship…"

38   Menta, "…Vulnerability and That Peach Scene."

39   Lee, Ashley. 2017. "Why Luca Guadagnino Didn't
Include Gay Actors or Explicit Sex Scenes in 'Call Me by
Your Name' (Q&A)." *The Hollywood Reporter*. February
8, 2017. https://www.hollywoodreporter.com/news/
call-me-by-your-name-why-luca-guadagnino-left-gay-
actors-explicit-sex-scenes-q-a-973256.

40   Blum, "The Queer Kids Who…"

41   Leschi, Julia Elia. n.d. "Don't Call Off 'Call Me By Your
Name.'" *Washington Square News*. Accessed May 25, 2018.
https://www.nyunews.com/2018/02/04/2-5-ops-leschi/.

42   Ibid.

43   Ocean, Frank. 2018. "Timothée Chalamet by Frank
Ocean." *V*, February 5, 2018. https://vman.com/
article/timothee-chalamet-frank-ocean.

44   Mandle, Chris. 2018. "…Rebellion, Addiction and
Speaking out."

45   Sharf, Zack. 2018. "'Beautiful Boy' First Look: Timothée Chalamet Eyes Another Oscar Nomination as Meth-Addicted Teen." *IndieWire*. March 22, 2018. http://www.indiewire.com/2018/03/beautiful-boy-first-look-timo-thee-chalamet-oscars-meth-teen-1201942796/.

46   Farrow, Dylan. 2014. "An Open Letter From Dylan Farrow." *The New York Times*, February 1, 2014.

47   Farrow, Dylan. 2017. "Dylan Farrow: Why Has the #MeToo Revolution Spared Woody Allen?" *Los Angeles Times*, December 7, 2017. http://www.latimes.com/opinion/op-ed/la-oe-farrow-woody-allen-me-too-20171207-story.html.

48   Rao, Sonia. 2018. "Colin Firth, Rachel Brosnahan Are the Latest Actors Who Won't Work with Woody Allen." *The Washington Post*, January 16, 2018. https://www.washingtonpost.com/news/arts-and-entertainment/wp/2018/01/16/timothee-chalamet-is-just-the-latest-actor-who-wont-work-with-woody-allen/.

49   "Hollywood Finally Disowns Woody Allen." 2018. *New York Post* "Page Six." January 27, 2018. https://pagesix.com/2018/01/27/woody-allens-rainy-day-in-new-york-might-not-get-released/.

50   "Woody Allen Offers Small Update On A Rainy Day In New York - The Woody Allen Pages." 2018. The Woody Allen Pages. May 8, 2018. http://www.woody-allenpages.com/2018/05/woody-allen-offers-small-up-date-on-a-rainy-day-in-new-york/.

51   Galanes, Philip. 2018. "How to Come of Age Onscreen? Saoirse Ronan and Timothée Chalamet Know." *The New York Times*. January 31, 2018. https://www.

nytimes.com/2018/01/31/arts/saoirse-ronan-timothee-
chalamet-lady-bird-call-me-by-your-name.html.

ABOUT THE AUTHOR

Damien Carlisle is a cinephile, history buff, and voracious reader of all genres. He enjoys bike riding, playing guitar, and painting rocks and hiding them in nature. He lives in a box-shaped house in the wilds of Kentucky with two dogs, four chickens, and a turtle.